Let's Dance

Let's Dance

Lyndon Wainwright

with Lynda King

Collins

This book is dedicated to my wife, Yvonne, for her understanding and patience while I was closeted away doing the solitary thing that writing is, and to my first wife, Felicia, without whom this book would not have been possible.

LYNDON WAINWRIGHT

Page 2: Ballroom dancing couple in formal attire performing a Waltz.

First published in 2005 by
Collins, an imprint of
HarperCollins*Publishers*
77-85 Fulham Palace Road
Hammersmith, London W6 8JB

The Collins website address is:
www.collins.co.uk

Collins is a registered trademark of HarperCollins Publishers Limited

09 08 07 06 05
6 5 4 3 2 1

Text © Lyndon Wainwright, 2005

Design, step-by-step photographs and illustrations © HarperCollins*Publishers*, 2005

Photographs © Advertising Archives, BBC, British Rail, Corbis, David Garten, Getty Images, The Kobal Collection, Lebrecht Music & Arts, Lyndon Wainwright, 2005 (see also Acknowledgements on page 256)

Lyndon Wainwright asserts the moral right to be identified as the author of this work.

A catalogue record for this book is available from the British Library

Created by: m&n publishing
Editor: Nina Sharman
Designer: Martin Hendry
Photographer: Christopher H. D. Davis
Illustrator: Lee Woodgate
Dance consultant: Lynda King
Stylist: Louise Sykes

CD production
Music arranged by Ross Mitchell of Dance and Listen Limited
Mastered by Isis Duplicating Co Limited
Produced by Deluxe Media Services

ISBN: 0 00 721280 1

Colour reproduction by Dot Gradations, UK
Printed and bound by LEGO S.p.A., Italy

Contents

Shall We Dance?

This couple are dancing the Tango – a physically challenging dance not only requiring strength but also balance.

Introduction

You may not have been aware of it, but dancing is in your blood and heritage. Naturally, throughout the years dances have changed according to circumstances. But the fact that dancing is in your psyche may not be, in itself, enough to get you dancing. We live in an age when life is full of labour-saving devices and many of us use a car to get about rather than walking or cycling. Thus the need to indulge in some exercise to keep fit becomes ever more important. Dancing can play an important and vital role for many in this need to improve one's physical health.

Not only does dancing help in maintaining a healthy body but it is also good for keeping the brain active. Medical research has even suggested that those who engage in dancing are less likely to develop Alzheimer's Disease. The discipline of learning the steps and applying them is invaluable to all, but perhaps most of all to the older person.

These are good enough reasons for one to dance but they pale into insignificance when one considers the joy of dancing. Movement to music is an instinctive natural response. Who has not felt the blood stirring or felt a lump in their throat when they hear a military march? When one responds to music in harmony with a partner, that instinctive enjoyment increases greatly. As one progresses with the dances and the movement becomes more fluent, another even greater joy becomes apparent in the flow of the dance with the music.

Forget the fancy steps that you may have seen experienced dancers perform, the basic joy comes from simple steps danced with the feeling of floating around the room. This will not come at once, but as your abilities improve a world you may not have imagined will open up for you.

Lyndon

LYNDON WAINWRIGHT

Lyndon Wainwright and his partner Deirdre Baker in a one-off performance of the Rumba.

The History of Dancing

It is little wonder that you would like to dance. Dancing in various forms has existed since before 10,000 BC. Palaeolithic man made drawings of men and women dancing together on the wall in a cave in Cogul in Northern Spain. Of course, the dances they performed were not those of today but they were typical of dances still used by native peoples throughout the world.

Not only did humans dance there is plenty of evidence that animals danced as well. Some apes are known to dance around tall, firmly fixed central objects in a pattern not unlike that of maypole dances.

Dance was an important aspect of ancient life. In the heyday of Grecian life it was an essential part of the training of Greek soldiers. In Britain, there is the tradition of Morris dancing that many think originated in ritual dances dating from the pre-Christian era. All such dances were performed by members of the same sex, outdoors and with participants wearing the heavy footwear of the time. Certainly dancing, involving both sexes, did not appear until the 15th century. Additionally, the advent of better flooring and lighter shoes enabled dances to move from the country setting into large indoor rooms.

Until the late 19th century dancing was an art demanded of courtiers. Queen Elizabeth I was an excellent dancer and there is a famous painting at Penshurst Palace in Kent said to be of her dancing the Volta, a popular dance of the time, with the Earl of Leicester. It is of especial interest because the Volta was one of the first, if not the first, dance in which dancers paired off in couples, and were not an integral part of a dance requiring several couples who would perform floor patterns needing one another.

By the end of the 19th century popular dancing, seen at the so-called assemblies of the day, comprised three forms of dance. One type consisted of dances, such as the Waltz and Polka, danced by couples. A second form of dance, for example, the Veleta and Military Two-Step, was enjoyed by all in unison to set sequences. While a third group consisted of dances, such as the Lancers and Quadrilles, where several couples danced patterns involving interchanging of couples and even partners. It is interesting to note that the Lancers could be

In the 16th century, the Volta became popular in the Royal Courts of Western Europe. Here, courtiers are dancing the Volta at the May Day Ball at Windsor Castle in a scene from the 1953 film, *The Sword and the Rose*, the story of young Mary Tudor.

quite rowdy. In the popular 'kitchen Lancers', couples could circle so fast that the ladies, held by the men, were swept off their feet with bodies and legs lifted off and almost parallel to the floor.

World War I brought about a revolution in dance styles, and dances involving couples, where the man dictated what was happening, became fashionable. Body contact between the couple became a necessity. The social foxtrot had mass appeal and the more elegant, sophisticated, and more difficult, slow foxtrot became the favoured dance of experienced dancers. Line dances in one form or another have always been enjoyed and after World War I the Palais Glide, then the Lambeth Walk and Hokey Cokey were hugely popular. The Cokey in the name is supposed to be a slang reference to cocaine.

After World War II and particularly in the 1950s there was another dance revolution. Rock 'n' roll was established and remains popular to this day. Then, in 1960, solo dancing in the form of the Twist by Chubby Checker was introduced to the ballroom.

In the 21st century, Latin dances have come much more to the fore and, in addition to the Rumba,

Samba, Salsa and Tango, dances such as the Lambada, Merengue and Mambo can be seen in dance competitions as well as on the dance floor.

While recent trends include street dancing, many dance schools include traditional belly dancing in their curriculum. Today there is an enormous range of dances to be found and those that survive for years to come will be those that the public adopt.

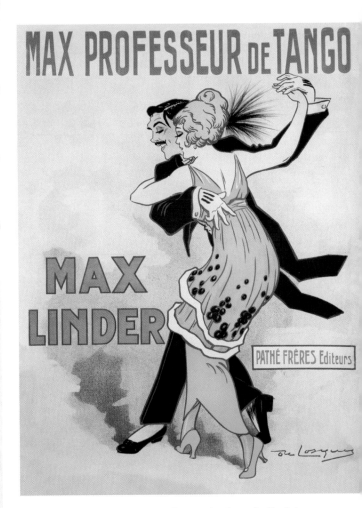

A poster by the artist Daniel de Losque, c.1916, advertising Max Linder's Tango dancing classes. The lady's empire line dress seems to be somewhat restrictive for such a physical dance.

Score cover (sheet music) of 'Starry Blue Night' by Ernesto Lecuona, composed in 1932.

Dance and Music

We are accustomed to thinking of dancing as being something performed to music but at its most elementary any rhythmic beat will suffice. The ticking of a metronome could do as a basis for dance steps. Of course, while the metronome does give a rhythm, it lacks any variety and expression. The rhythm section of an orchestra produces a great variety of moods and expression. The melody complements the rhythms giving more depth and colour to any musical piece.

THE RHYTHM From the point of view of the dance beginner it is the rhythm that is all important and that he or she must listen for. All the dances you will meet in the book are in 4/4, 3/4 or 2/4 time. The only one in 3/4 time is the Waltz. Play track 2 on the CD and listen for the regular heavy beat followed by another heavy beat about two seconds later. You should be able to hear two less pronounced beats filling the space between the heavy beats. Count 'one' on the heavy beat and then 'two, three', on the next two less well-pronounced beats and this is the count for three steps in waltz time.

The other sorts of music are in 4/4 or 2/4 time. In either case you can count two slows or four quicks in a bar of music. In most such music the beats are of more even emphasis than those of the waltz. Much pop music has very pronounced beats indeed and

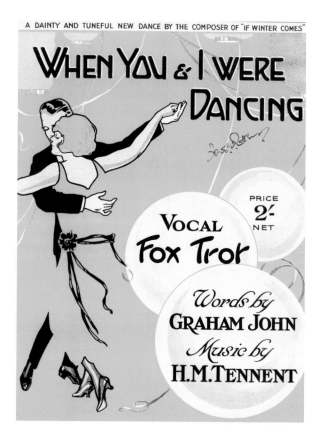

Score cover (sheet music) of 'When You And I Were Dancing', a vocal foxtrot.

Let's Dance CD

Music determines what style of dance you are going to perform. The CD that accompanies this book contains some ideal music for the various dances included. As Disco can be danced to a very wide range of readily available music, none is provided here.

Foxtrot
'Getting To Know You' (Rodgers, Hammerstein)

Waltz
'Sam' (Farrar, Marvin, Black)

Cha Cha Cha
'Pata Pata' (Makeba, Ragovoy)

Quickstep
'Diamonds Are A Girl's Best Friend' (Robin, Styne)

Rock 'n' Roll/Jive
'Runaround Sue' (Di Mucci, Maresca)

Samba
'Iko Iko' (Hawkins, Hawkins, Johnson, Thomas, Jones, Jones, Jones)

Salsa
'She Knows That She Wants To' (Weimar, Wilson)

Tango
'Perfidia' (Dominguez)

Rumba
'Can You Feel The Love Tonight?' (John, Rice)

can often be felt through the floor as well as heard. Generally the first and third beat of the four are more pronounced than the second and fourth. You should be able to hear the four beats and the pronounced beats should also be fairly obvious.

This is all you need to worry about at this stage. However, for any more musically literate of you we should mention that sometimes the second and fourth beats in a bar are more heavily accented than the first and third. Such music is ideal for Rock 'n' Roll. The Latin dances, for instance, Rumba and Cha Cha Cha, and those influenced by Latin dance such as Salsa, often have very complex and intricate variations to the basic rhythm. Nevertheless, the basic 4/4 count is not lost and the complications of the Cuban influence need not worry you.

Twin-kle, twin-kle, lit - tle star, How I won-der what you are

In the first of these four bars of music from the popular nursery rhyme, each 'twinkle' takes two musical crotchets that is two 'Quick' counts. In bar two 'little' takes two Quicks and 'star' (clearly longer) takes a 'Slow'.

Dancers take to the floor to enjoy a formal band. In the 1950s the standard dance band comprised fourteen musicians: one on violin, four on rhythm, four on saxophones and five on brass.

Dress Code

The dances in this book are ballroom dances. Nowadays, there are not as many ballrooms as once there were. However, there are still many places where dancing takes place including hotels, clubs, public halls and some larger dance schools.

WHAT SHOULD YOU WEAR? As regards dress for both lady and man, this will be dictated by the venue and style of the dance. However, whatever you wear should be comfortable and appropriate for the particular type of dance. It should not be too restricting especially around the legs for the ladies. As you will see from the notes relating to moving dances on page 17, it is important for many dances that you are able to swing the legs freely from the hips without any restriction.

Obviously shoes are of vital importance. They should be lightweight and with a flexible sole, if possible a leather sole. Good dancers use shoes with special 'non-skid' soles made of chrome leather or similar but at the beginner level this is not necessary. However, the sole of the shoes should not impede movement of the foot across the floor in steps where you stroke the floor with the feet. Ladies should wear a shoe with a heel. This will assist that all-important balance on backwards steps in ballroom, especially when the lady has more steps than the man.

A young couple jiving in 1956 at a dance competition in London. 'Off-beat', informal clothing – leopard-skin jeans and bare feet for her, jeans and rolled-up sleeves for him – reflects the style of dance they are performing.

Wearing accessories, such as this choker, can give your outfit a touch of elegance.

Women should wear shoes that have 'non-skid' soles and avoid stiletto heels in order to aid balance and avoid falling.

An immaculately groomed Lyndon and Felicia Wainwright strike a pose after dancing the Samba. The formal attire they are wearing is in stark contrast to that in the above picture.

How to Use this Book

In this book the popular modern dances are introduced, with the assumption that readers are complete novices. The figures (or the routines) taught in each dance have been chosen to get you up and dancing as soon as possible. Many of them are simplified versions of more sophisticated figures in the hope that the experience and joy of dancing and moving to music will encourage you to delve a little more deeply. A visit to a local school of dance will broaden your horizons immensely. As with all disciplines a jargon has grown up around dance analysis and here it is used only if it provides a useful shortcut to learning. All dance parlance is explained in the Glossary on page 248.

Since each dance is described on the basis that you have no previous knowledge, you can start with any dance. However, because it can be danced to such a wide variety of music, it might be helpful to start with the Foxtrot – a dance that beginners can easily learn and enjoy. After that the choice is yours.

Dances comprise individual figures that are joined together, in some cases one after another. Suggestions for grouping figures together are given here.

Start positions for both the man and the lady are given for the ballroom dances that move in an anti-clockwise direction, except when one figure follows another.

On the foot diagrams, start positions for the man and the lady are given for all figures. Note that the pale foot is the left and the dark foot the right.

When you see a dotted foot, it means that you move your foot slightly after you have taken the main step.

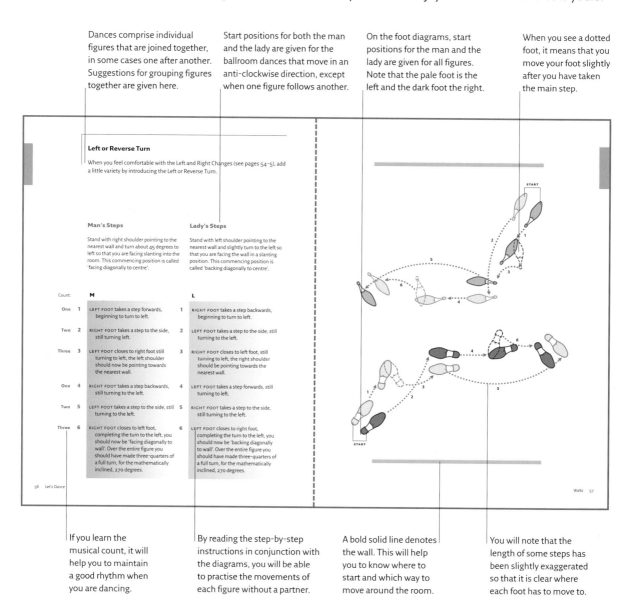

Left or Reverse Turn

When you feel comfortable with the Left and Right Changes (see pages 54–5), add a little variety by introducing the Left or Reverse Turn.

Man's Steps

Stand with right shoulder pointing to the nearest wall and turn about 45 degrees to left so that you are facing slanting into the room. This commencing position is called 'facing diagonally to centre'.

Lady's Steps

Stand with left shoulder pointing to the nearest wall and slightly turn to the left so that you are facing the wall in a slanting position. This commencing position is called 'backing diagonally to centre'.

Count:	M		L	
One	1	LEFT FOOT takes a step forwards, beginning to turn to left.	1	RIGHT FOOT takes a step backwards, beginning to turn to left.
Two	2	RIGHT FOOT takes a step to the side, still turning left.	2	LEFT FOOT takes a step to the side, still turning to the left.
Three	3	LEFT FOOT closes to right foot still turning to left, the left shoulder should now be pointing towards the nearest wall.	3	RIGHT FOOT closes to left foot, still turning to the left, the right shoulder should now be pointing towards the nearest wall.
One	4	RIGHT FOOT takes a step backwards, still turning to the left.	4	LEFT FOOT takes a step forwards, still turning to left.
Two	5	LEFT FOOT takes a step to the side, still turning to the left.	5	RIGHT FOOT takes a step to the side, still turning to the left.
Three	6	RIGHT FOOT closes to left foot, completing the turn to the left, you should now be 'facing diagonally to wall'. Over the entire figure you should have made three-quarters of a full turn, for the mathematically inclined, 270 degrees.	6	LEFT FOOT closes to right foot, completing the turn to the left, you should now be 'backing diagonally to wall'. Over the entire figure you should have made three-quarters of a full turn, for the mathematically inclined, 270 degrees.

START

START

56   Let's Dance

Waltz   57

If you learn the musical count, it will help you to maintain a good rhythm when you are dancing.

By reading the step-by-step instructions in conjunction with the diagrams, you will be able to practise the movements of each figure without a partner.

A bold solid line denotes the wall. This will help you to know where to start and which way to move around the room.

You will note that the length of some steps has been slightly exaggerated so that it is clear where each foot has to move to.

Although it is not essential, all figures for couples start on the man's left and the lady's right foot. This helps overcome some of the uncertainty beginners have at the very start of a dance.

FOOT DIAGRAMS In each figure, foot diagrams of the steps are included as an aid to following the instructions (see opposite). While these are as accurate as possible, in some cases it has been necessary to exaggerate the size of the steps in order to avoid having too many on the same point.

FEET AND LEGS The way we use our feet and legs in dancing is important and becomes more so as we advance in ability. It is wise to try to establish the correct use right at the beginning and so avoid having to make adjustments later.

With the exception of Tango, the various dances described fall into one of two categories. The first includes the moving dances, such as the Waltz and Quickstep. The second mostly includes the non-moving Latin dances, for example, Salsa and Rumba, plus the dances that have developed for use when the floor space is limited, for instance Foxtrot (also known as Rhythm Dancing).

MOVING DANCES In the moving dances most forwards steps, taken by either the man or lady, are similar to walking and taken on the heel of the stepping foot. You should think of the leg as a pendulum with the foot as the bob weight. The leg swings from the hips with the foot lightly skimming the floor rather than bending the knee and picking the foot up and placing it forwards. The leg swing, plus some leverage from the static foot, creates the sort of movement which you are striving for, once you have learnt the step patterns. As you move forwards the heel of the supporting foot should peel off the floor giving additional leverage to the forwards momentum.

On backwards steps, you should try to straighten the ankle so that you are reaching backwards with the toes. This is important for the vital area of control, and this will appeal to beginners, as it helps to keep the feet out of your partner's way and will prevent you from getting trodden on.

NON-MOVING DANCES In the non-moving dances all steps at beginner level are taken on the ball of the foot with the heel settling to the floor immediately after the foot is in position. The hips settle to the left and right according to the steps, and the amount of pressure placed into the floor on the supporting foot is essential in achieving this. This is a crucial characteristic of most Latin dances.

In the first figure of each dance, the beat of music is given. This beat applies to all other figures unless otherwise stated.

The step-by-step photographs generally show the position you and your partner will be in at the end of each instruction.

The Left Side Basic

One *Two* *Three* *Four*

1 **M** LEFT FOOT to side, leg straightens, weight on foot, swing hips to left.
L RIGHT FOOT to side, leg straightens, weight on foot, swing hips to right.

2 **M** RIGHT FOOT closes towards left foot, swing hips to the right.
L LEFT FOOT closes towards right foot, leg straightens, swing hips to the left.

3 **M** LEFT FOOT to the side, without putting full weight onto the foot.
L RIGHT FOOT to the side, without putting full weight onto the foot.

4 **M** LEFT LEG straightens, swing hips to the left and tap right toes.
L RIGHT LEG straightens, swing hips to the right and tap left toes.

Cucaracha Steps

One *Two* *Three* *Four*

1 **M** LEFT FOOT to the side, retain pressure on right foot, swing hips to left.
L RIGHT FOOT to the side, retain some pressure on left foot, swing hips to right.

2 **M** LEFT FOOT pushes off against the floor, weight onto right foot, swing hips to right.
L RIGHT FOOT pushes off against the floor, weight onto left foot, hips to left.

3 **M** LEFT FOOT closes to right foot, taking the weight onto left foot.
L RIGHT FOOT closes to left foot, taking the weight onto right foot.

4 **M** RIGHT FOOT lifts just off the floor with a flick action.
L LEFT FOOT lifts just off the floor with a flick action.

176   Let's Dance

The man's and lady's instructions here are slightly abridged versions of those that accompany the foot diagrams. They read from left to right across two pages in most instances.

Dance Holds and Positions

There are three basic holds used for the dances in this book.

CUDDLE HOLD (SOCIAL DANCE) Both man and lady should stand up well, facing each other and in a relaxed position avoiding tension. The lady's right hip should contact the man roughly midway across his body. The man's right hand and arm go well round the lady so his hand rests under her right shoulder. Keep the fingers of the right hand close together and bent not straight. The lady rests her left hand on the man's shoulder and if the mood takes her can go round the man's neck. The man holds the lady's right hand in his left with his fingers across the knuckles of the lady's hand. (Hands can be held level with his neck, with his left elbow away from the body so that the angle at the elbow is preferably less than 45 degrees and certainly not much more.) The most important thing is you should try to feel comfortable, and don't be afraid to adjust the hold until you do.

CLOSE HOLD (BALLROOM) This is a body contact hold but less relaxed than the cuddle hold described above. Both man and lady should stand up well with the lady's right hip roughly midway between the man's hips. Without being too military about it the man should stand erect and the lady should lean back slightly from the hips upwards. Don't overdo this backwards lean. The man holds the lady with his right hand on her back just below her left shoulder blade. According to your relative sizes the man should make rather less than a right angle at his right elbow. The lady rests her left hand on the man's upper arm just below the shoulder. The man needs to hold the lady firmly without overdoing the pressure and holding the lady's right in his left hand with his fingers and thumb spanning the breadth of

The Cuddle Hold is used mostly in social dancing and can be very relaxed.

The Close Hold is the stance adopted for many ballroom dances.

The Open Hold is the classic one used for Latin dancing.

the lady's hand. Good dancers hold hands fairly high but to start with the man's left hand should be about level with his chin and neck. Both elbows should be at the same height.

OPEN HOLD (LATIN) Stand about 15–20 cm (6–8 in) away from each other. The man holds the lady with his right hand on her back just below her left shoulder blade and with the heel of his hand almost on the side of the lady's body. He holds her right hand loosely in his left hand at a little below shoulder level or lower. The lady will rest her left hand on the upper part of the man's right arm. The main thing is to find a hold around this description that you find comfortable. As in all dances where body contact is not the norm, there will be occasions where the man will release hold of his partner with either his left or right hand. When this occurs, it will be described in the text.

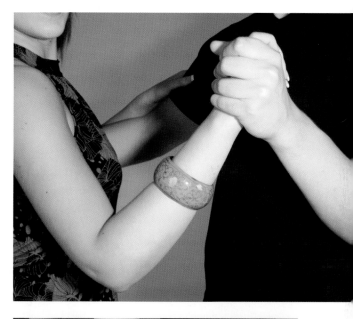

Dancers demonstrate the positioning of hands for Latin dances, such as the Rumba.

This hand positioning is used in ballroom dancing, for instance in the Waltz.

Dancers' feet in promenade position. This occurs in many dances. The man's left and lady's right sides are turned away from one another allowing them both to step forwards with the man's right and the lady's left foot.

A dancer demonstrates the Latin cross, which is used in the Rumba and Cha Cha Cha.

Foxtrot

A ballroom masterclass: Fred Astaire and Ginger Rogers dancing the Foxtrot, 1933.

The Foxtrot is named after an American actor, Harry Fox, whose real name was Arthur Carringford; he called himself Fox after his grandfather, who was a celebrated clown.

NORTHERN COUNTIES HOTEL

PORTRUSH

NORTHERN IRELAND

an **L M S HOTEL**
(NORTHERN COUNTIES COMMITTEE)

FOR TARIFF PARTICULARS APPLY TO RESIDENT MANAGER.

A British Rail poster, *c*.1920, for Portrush, a sophisticated, grand hotel in Northern Ireland. Like other elegant hotels of the period, Portrush organized ballroom dances for their guests and visitors.

As part of his vaudeville act Harry Fox performed a comic walk, accompanied by ragtime music, which became known as 'Fox's Trot'. In April 1914, Harry was presenting his act as part of a theatrical interlude in between films at Hammerstein's – a movie house that had been converted from one of the largest theatres in the world. There was a roof garden above the theatre, called the 'Jardin de Danse', and the management wanted to promote Harry and exploit his 'Fox's Trot', so they included it in the dance repetoire for the general public in the roof garden. The name has lived on as Foxtrot.

This is the most universally popular dance for couples. It can be danced to any music in 4/4 (common) time and the speed of the music is not a determining factor. The Foxtrot is a dance in which partners keep close contact with each other and do not move a great deal and is known by many names such as 'crush dancing', 'social foxtrot', 'café style', 'American foxtrot'. The names tell you a great deal about the dance. Any time you see the general public dancing in a film and the music is in common time this is the dance most of the couples will be doing.

As you will see in the Left Box (see pages 24–5) some steps take two beats and some one. Any mental count that helps you remember the steps and keep in time with the music is acceptable.

THE HOLD AND LEADING In this dance you use the Cuddle Hold (see page 18). The man leads or guides the lady through the figures and, as the name implies, you do not take long steps in this dance. It is important that you maintain the body contact because this is where the lead originates. The man can help by holding the lady close to him with his right hand, but don't forget she does need to breathe. The lady needs to try and keep relaxed and not to fight against the lead that comes from the man. If the mood takes the lady and she wants to nestle her head on her partner's shoulder and snuggle up to him, well, why not?

Denise Lewis and Ian Waite show off their Foxtrot in the second series of BBC TV's *Strictly Come Dancing*. In the series, celebrities teamed up with dance experts and then went on to compete against each other.

The Left Box

Learn the following steps solo but as soon as possible try them with a partner. Do not try to stride out too much. Steps taken forwards and backwards should be just be a little shorter than normal walking steps and side steps about, say, two shoe widths. When you have a partner, place your hands on his or her shoulders so that you can see how the steps follow each other. As soon as both of you are confident with the step pattern, stand close to one another with bodies touching at the hips. The man should hold the lady firmly so that she can feel him placing the weight onto his right foot and that should indicate to her to settle her weight onto her left foot.

Man's Steps

Start by facing the nearest wall. Take the weight onto your right foot so that, while your left foot remains in contact with the floor, it is free to move without having to make any weight change.

Lady's Steps

Start with your back to the nearest wall. Take the weight onto your left foot so that, while your right foot remains in contact with the floor, it is free to move without having to make any weight change.

Count:		M		L
Slow	1	LEFT FOOT takes a step forwards, taking two beats of music.	1	RIGHT FOOT takes a step backwards, taking two beats of music.
Quick	2	RIGHT FOOT takes a step to the side on the same line as left foot, taking one beat of music.	2	LEFT FOOT takes a step to the side, on the same line as right foot, taking one beat of music.
Quick	3	LEFT FOOT closes to right foot, transferring weight onto left foot, and taking one beat of music.	3	RIGHT FOOT closes to left foot, transferring weight onto right foot and taking one beat of music.
Slow	4	RIGHT FOOT takes a step backwards, taking two beats of music.	4	LEFT FOOT takes a step forwards, taking two beats of music.
Quick	5	LEFT FOOT takes a step to the side on the same line as right foot, taking one beat of music.	5	RIGHT FOOT takes a step to the side on the same line as left foot, taking one beat of music.
Quick	6	RIGHT FOOT closes to left foot, transferring weight onto right foot and taking one beat of music.	6	LEFT FOOT closes to right foot, transferring weight onto left foot and taking one beat of music.

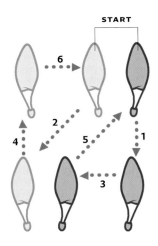

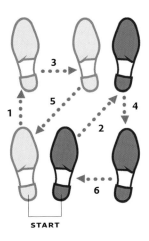

The Left Box with Left Turn

Once you are happy that you have mastered the foot pattern of the Left Box then you can add turns to the figure.

Man's Steps

Start by facing the nearest wall and on all steps, turn a little to your left.

Lady's Steps

Start with your back to the nearest wall and on all steps, turn a little to your left.

Count:		M		L
Slow	1	LEFT FOOT takes a step forwards, turning to the left, that is, bringing the right side of your body forwards as you step and taking two beats of music.	1	RIGHT FOOT takes a step backwards, turning to the left and taking two beats of music.
Quick	2	RIGHT FOOT takes a step to the side, still turning to the left and taking one beat of music.	2	LEFT FOOT takes a step to the side, still turning to the left and taking one beat of music.
Quick	3	LEFT FOOT closes to right foot, still turning to the left and taking one beat of music.	3	RIGHT FOOT closes to left foot, still turning to the left and taking one beat of music.
Slow	4	RIGHT FOOT takes a step backwards, still turning to the left, that is, bringing the left side of your body backwards and taking two beats of music.	4	LEFT FOOT takes a step forwards, still turning to the left and taking two beats of music.
Quick	5	LEFT FOOT takes a step to the side, still turning to the left and taking one beat of music.	5	RIGHT FOOT takes a step to the side, still turning to the left and taking one beat of music.
Quick	6	RIGHT FOOT closes to left foot, still turning to the left and taking one beat of music.	6	LEFT FOOT closes to right foot, still turning to the left and taking one beat of music.

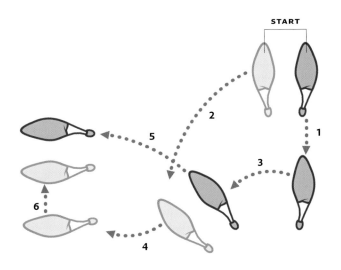

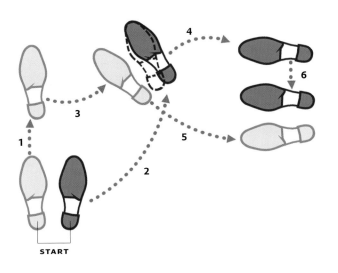

The Foxtrot is a dance in which partners keep close contact with each other and do not move a great deal. Anytime you see dancing in a film or on television, if the music is in common time, this is the dance most of the couples will be doing.

The Left Box

Slow

1 **M** LEFT FOOT takes a step forwards.
L RIGHT FOOT takes a step backwards.
Takes two beats of music.

Quick

2 **M** RIGHT FOOT takes a step to the side on the same line as left foot.
L LEFT FOOT takes a step to the side, on the same line as right foot. Takes one beat of music.

Quick

3 **M** LEFT FOOT closes to right foot, transferring weight onto foot.
L RIGHT FOOT closes to left foot, transferring weight onto foot.
Takes one beat of music.

Slow

4 **M** RIGHT FOOT takes a step backwards.
L LEFT FOOT takes a step forwards.
Takes two beats of music.

Quick

5 **M** LEFT FOOT takes a step to the side on the same line as right foot.
L RIGHT FOOT takes a step to the side on the same line as left foot. Takes one beat of music.

Quick

6 **M** RIGHT FOOT closes to left foot, transferring weight onto foot.
L LEFT FOOT closes to right foot, transferring weight onto foot.
Takes one beat of music.

The Right Box

The preparatory side (weight change) step has been introduced so that both the man and the lady always start on the same foot. Steps 1–6 (inclusive) of the Right Box can be repeated.

Man's Steps

Start by standing erect, in close body contact with your partner and facing the nearest wall. As a result of the preparatory step to your left side, you will be free to move off with your right foot into the Right Box itself.

Lady's Steps

Start by standing erect, in close body contact with your partner and backing the nearest wall. As a result of the preparatory step to your right side, you will be free to move off with your left foot when you feel the man move off with his right foot.

Count:		**M**		**L**
Slow	P	LEFT FOOT takes a small step to the side, taking two beats of music.	P	RIGHT FOOT takes a small step to the side, taking two beats of music.
Slow	1	RIGHT FOOT takes a step forwards, taking two beats of music.	1	LEFT FOOT takes a step backwards, taking two beats of music.
Quick	2	LEFT FOOT takes a step to the side onto the same line as right foot, taking one beat of music.	2	RIGHT FOOT takes a step to the side on the same line as left foot, taking one beat of music.
Quick	3	RIGHT FOOT closes to left foot, transferring weight onto right foot and taking one beat of music.	3	LEFT FOOT closes to right foot, transferring weight onto left foot and taking one beat of music.
Slow	4	LEFT FOOT takes a step backwards, taking two beats of music.	4	RIGHT FOOT takes a step forwards, taking two beats of music.
Quick	5	RIGHT FOOT takes a step to the side onto the same line as left foot, taking one beat of music.	5	LEFT FOOT takes a step to the side onto the same line as right foot, taking one beat of music.
Quick	6	LEFT FOOT closes to right foot, transferring weight onto left foot and taking one beat of music.	6	RIGHT FOOT closes to left foot, transferring weight onto right foot and taking one beat of music.

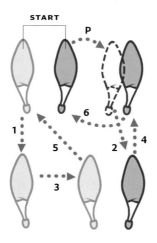

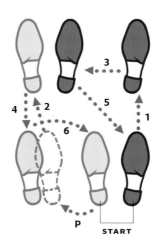

The Right Box with Right Turn

The Right Box with Right Turn comprises steps 1–6 omitting the preparatory step. Steps 1 to 6 (inclusive) can be repeated.

Man's Steps

Start by facing the nearest wall.

Lady's Steps

Start with your back to the nearest wall.

Count:		M		L
Slow	P	LEFT FOOT takes a small step to the side, taking two beats of music.	P	RIGHT FOOT takes a small step to the side, taking two beats of music.
Slow	1	RIGHT FOOT takes a step forwards, turning to the right, that is, bringing the left side of your body forwards as you step and taking two beats of music.	1	LEFT FOOT takes a step backwards, turning to the right and taking two beats of music.
Quick	2	LEFT FOOT takes a step to the side, still turning to the right and taking one beat of music.	2	RIGHT FOOT takes a step to the side, still turning to the right and taking one beat of music.
Quick	3	RIGHT FOOT closes to left foot, still turning to the right and taking one beat of music.	3	LEFT FOOT closes to right foot, still turning to the right and taking one beat of music.
Slow	4	LEFT FOOT takes a step backwards, still turning to the right, that is, bringing the right side of your body backwards and taking two beats of music.	4	RIGHT FOOT takes a step forwards, still turning to the right and taking two beats of music.
Quick	5	RIGHT FOOT takes a step to the side, still turning to the right and taking one beat of music.	5	LEFT FOOT takes a step to the side, still turning to the right, taking one beat of music.
Quick	6	LEFT FOOT closes to right foot, still turning to the right and taking one beat of music.	6	RIGHT FOOT closes to left foot, still turning to the right and taking one beat of music.

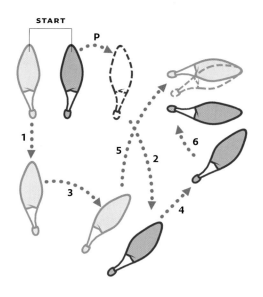

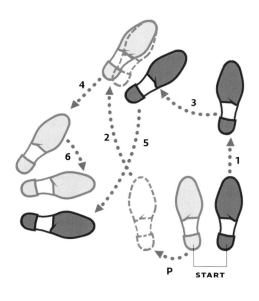

The Right Box

Slow

Slow

Quick

Quick

P **M** LEFT FOOT takes a small step to the side.
L RIGHT FOOT takes a small step to the side.
Takes two beats of music.

1 **M** RIGHT FOOT takes a step forwards.
L LEFT FOOT takes a step backwards.
Takes two beats of music.

2 **M** LEFT FOOT takes a step to the side onto the same line as right foot.
L RIGHT FOOT takes a step to the side on the same line as left foot.
Takes one beat of music.

3 **M** RIGHT FOOT closes to left foot, transferring weight onto right foot.
L LEFT FOOT closes to right foot, transferring weight onto left foot.
Takes one beat of music.

The Right Box with Right Turn

Slow

Slow

Quick

P **M** LEFT FOOT takes a small step to the side.
L RIGHT FOOT takes a small step to the side.
Takes two beats of music.

1 **M** RIGHT FOOT takes a step forwards, turning to the right.
L LEFT FOOT takes a step backwards, turning to the right.
Takes two beats of music.

2 **M** LEFT FOOT takes a step to the side, still turning to the right.
L RIGHT FOOT takes a step to the side, still turning to the right.
Takes one beat of music.

Slow

Quick

Quick

4 **M** LEFT FOOT takes a step backwards.
L RIGHT FOOT takes a step forwards.
Takes two beats of music.

5 **M** RIGHT FOOT takes a step to side onto same line as left foot.
L LEFT FOOT takes a step to side onto the same line as right foot.
Takes one beat of music.

6 **M** LEFT FOOT closes to right foot, transferring weight onto left foot.
L RIGHT FOOT closes to left foot, transferring weight onto right foot.
Takes one beat of music.

Quick

Slow

Quick

Quick

3 **M** RIGHT FOOT closes to left foot, still turning to the right.
L LEFT FOOT closes to right foot, still turning to the right.
Takes one beat of music.

4 **M** LEFT FOOT takes a step backwards, still turning to the right.
L RIGHT FOOT takes a step forwards, still turning to the right.
Takes two beats of music.

5 **M** RIGHT FOOT takes a step to the side, still turning to the right.
L LEFT FOOT takes a step to the side, still turning to the right.
Takes one beat of music.

6 **M** LEFT FOOT closes to right foot, still turning to the right.
L RIGHT FOOT closes to left foot, still turning to the right.
Takes one beat of music.

The Progressive Boxes

Once you have mastered the two basic turns you will need to amalgamate them. Dance the preparatory step and steps 1–6 of the Right Box with Right Turn. Follow with steps 4–6 of the Left Box with Left Turn and then steps 1–3 of the Left Box with Left Turn. This sequence of 12 steps will take you around the room and can be repeated as many times as you wish. Remember that the slow count is two beats of music and the quick count one beat.

	Count:	**M**		**L**
Slow	P	LEFT FOOT takes a small step to the side.	P	RIGHT FOOT takes a small step to the side.
Slow	1	RIGHT FOOT takes a step forwards, turning to the right.	1	LEFT FOOT takes a step backwards, turning to the right.
Quick	2	LEFT FOOT takes a step to the side, still turning to the right.	2	RIGHT FOOT takes a step to the side, still turning to the right.
Quick	3	RIGHT FOOT closes to left foot, still turning to the right.	3	LEFT FOOT closes to right foot, still turning to the right.
Slow	4	LEFT FOOT takes a step backwards, still turning to the right.	4	RIGHT FOOT takes a step forwards, still turning to the right.
Quick	5	RIGHT FOOT takes a step to the side, still turning to the right.	5	LEFT FOOT takes a step to the side, still turning to the right.
Quick	6	LEFT FOOT closes to right foot, completing the right turn.	6	RIGHT FOOT closes to left foot, completing the right turn.
Slow	7	RIGHT FOOT takes a step backwards, turning to the left.	7	LEFT FOOT takes a step forwards, turning to the left.
Quick	8	LEFT FOOT takes a step to the side, still turning to the left.	8	RIGHT FOOT takes a step to the side, still turning to the left.
Quick	9	RIGHT FOOT closes to left foot, still turning to the left.	9	LEFT FOOT closes to right foot, still turning to the left.
Slow	10	LEFT FOOT takes a step forwards, still turning to the left.	10	RIGHT FOOT takes a step backwards, still turning to the left.
Quick	11	RIGHT FOOT takes a step to the side, still turning to the left.	11	LEFT FOOT takes a step to the side, still turning to the left.
Quick	12	LEFT FOOT closes to right foot, completing the left turn.	12	RIGHT FOOT closes to left foot, completing the left turn.

Man's Steps

Start by 'facing diagonally to wall'.

Lady's Steps

Start by 'backing diagonally to wall'.

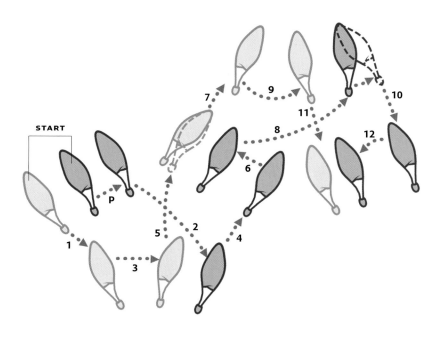

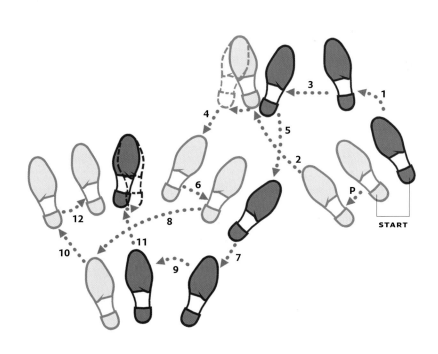

The Progressive Boxes

Slow   *Slow*   *Quick*

P   **M** LEFT FOOT takes a small step to the side.
L RIGHT FOOT takes a small step to the side.

1   **M** RIGHT FOOT takes a step forwards, turning to the right.
L LEFT FOOT takes a step backwards, turning to the right.

2   **M** LEFT FOOT takes a step to the side, turning to the right.
L RIGHT FOOT takes a step to the side, turning to the right.

Slow   *Quick*   *Quick*   *Slow*

7   **M** RIGHT FOOT takes a step backwards, turning to the left.
L LEFT FOOT takes a step forwards, turning to the left.

8   **M** LEFT FOOT takes a step to the side, turning to the left.
L RIGHT FOOT takes a step to the side, turning to the left.

9   **M** RIGHT FOOT closes to left foot, turning to the left.
L LEFT FOOT closes to right foot, turning to the left.

10   **M** LEFT FOOT takes a step forwards. turning to the left.
L RIGHT FOOT takes a step backwards, turning to the left.

Quick

Slow

Quick

Quick

3 **M** RIGHT FOOT closes to left foot, turning to the right.
L LEFT FOOT closes to right foot, turning to the right.

4 **M** LEFT FOOT takes a step backwards, turning to the right.
L RIGHT FOOT takes a step forwards, turning to the right.

5 **M** RIGHT FOOT takes a step to the side, turning to the right.
L LEFT FOOT takes a step to the side, turning to the right.

6 **M** LEFT FOOT closes to right foot, completing the right turn.
L RIGHT FOOT closes to left foot, completing the right turn.

Quick

Quick

11 **M** RIGHT FOOT takes a step to the side, turning to the left.
L LEFT FOOT takes a step to the side, turning to the left.

12 **M** LEFT FOOT closes to right foot, completing the left turn.
L RIGHT FOOT closes to left foot, completing the left turn.

Turning Technique

In the Progressive Boxes the man will turn to the right on the first six steps and to the left on the next six. The turns should be roughly equal so that at the end of the sequence the man is facing in the same direction as that in which he started, even though he and his partner have moved a little further around the room.

After step 12, the man steps forwards with his right foot to start the Progressive Boxes once again.

The Right Pivot Box

So far you have learnt the basic boxes both with and without turn and can join them together and progress around the room. A useful and pleasant variation on the Right Box is the Right Pivot Box.

You will see that this figure is merely the first four steps of the Right Box with Turn repeated, and steps 5–8 can be repeated as often as you wish.

		Man's Steps		Lady's Steps

Man's Steps

Start by 'facing diagonally to wall'.

Lady's Steps

Start by 'backing diagonally to wall'.

Count:		M		L
Slow	P	LEFT FOOT takes a small step to the side.	P	RIGHT FOOT takes a small step to the side.
Slow	1	RIGHT FOOT takes a step forwards, turning to the right.	1	LEFT FOOT takes a step backwards, turning to the right.
Quick	2	LEFT FOOT takes a step to the side, still turning to the right.	2	RIGHT FOOT takes a step to the side, still turning to the right.
Quick	3	RIGHT FOOT closes to left foot, still turning to the right.	3	LEFT FOOT closes to right foot, still turning to the right.
Slow	4	LEFT FOOT takes a step backwards, still turning to the right and checking backwards impetus.	4	RIGHT FOOT takes a step forwards, still turning to the right and responding to the man and checking his backwards impetus.
Slow	5	RIGHT FOOT takes a step slightly forwards, still turning to the right.	5	LEFT FOOT takes a step slightly backwards, still turning to the right.
Quick	6	LEFT FOOT takes a step to the side, still turning to the right.	6	RIGHT FOOT takes a step to the side, still turning to the right.
Quick	7	RIGHT FOOT closes to left foot, still turning to the right.	7	LEFT FOOT closes to right foot, still turning to the right.
Slow	8	LEFT FOOT takes a step backwards, still turning to the right and checking backwards impetus.	8	RIGHT FOOT takes a step forwards, still turning to the right and responding to the man and checking his backwards impetus.

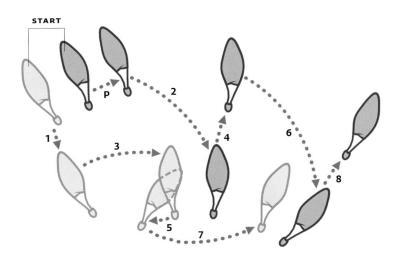

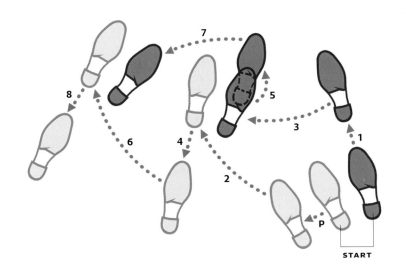

The Right Pivot Box

Slow

P **M** LEFT FOOT takes a small step to the side.
L RIGHT FOOT takes a small step to the side.

Slow

1 **M** RIGHT FOOT takes a step forwards, turning to the right.
L LEFT FOOT takes a step backwards, turning to the right.

Slow

5 **M** RIGHT FOOT takes a step slightly forwards, turning to the right.
L LEFT FOOT takes a step slightly backwards, turning to the right.

Quick

6 **M** LEFT FOOT takes a step to the side, turning to the right.
L RIGHT FOOT takes a step to the side, turning to the right.

Quick

7 **M** RIGHT FOOT closes to left foot, turning to the right.
L LEFT FOOT closes to right foot, turning to the right.

Quick

2 **M** LEFT FOOT takes a step to the side, turning to the right.
L RIGHT FOOT takes a step to the side, turning to the right.

Quick

3 **M** RIGHT FOOT closes to left foot, turning to the right.
L LEFT FOOT closes to right foot, turning to the right.

Slow

4 **M** LEFT FOOT takes a step backwards, turning to the right and checking backwards impetus.
L RIGHT FOOT takes a step forwards, turning to the right.

Slow

8 **M** LEFT FOOT takes a step backwards, turning to the right and checking backwards impetus.
L RIGHT FOOT takes a step forwards turning to the right.

In the Cuddle Hold, the man leads the lady through the figures and, as the name Foxtrot implies, you do not take long steps.

The Conversation Piece

This figure is preceded by the preparatory step and steps 1–4 of the Right Box with Right Turn (see pages 32–3). You can repeat steps 3–6 of the Conversation Piece as often as you wish before going into step 7. Once you have danced the Conversation Piece, follow it with either the Left Box or steps 4–6 of the Right Box.

Man's Steps

Lady's Steps

Count:		**M**		**L**
Quick	1	RIGHT FOOT takes a step to the side, increasing pressure on heel of right hand, indicating to partner that she has to turn her right side away from your left side.	1	LEFT FOOT takes a step to the side, turning to the right so that your right side turns away from the man's left side.
Quick	2	LEFT FOOT closes to right foot, still turning partner so that her right side is roughly 30 cm (11 ¾ in) away from your left side (in promenade position).	2	RIGHT FOOT closes to left foot, still turning so that your right side is roughly 30 cm (11 ¾ in) away from the man's left side (in promenade position).
Slow	3	RIGHT FOOT takes a step forwards and across left foot, partner is also stepping forwards through the space between her right and your left hips in promenade position.	3	LEFT FOOT takes a step forwards and across right foot, partner is also stepping forwards through the space between your right and his left hips in promenade position.
Quick	4	LEFT FOOT takes a step to the side and slightly forwards, still in promenade position.	4	RIGHT FOOT takes a step to the side and slightly forwards still in promenade position.
Quick	5	RIGHT FOOT closes to left foot, still in promenade position.	5	LEFT FOOT closes to right foot, still in promenade position.
Slow	6	LEFT FOOT takes a step to the side and slightly forwards, still in promenade position.	6	RIGHT FOOT takes a step to the side and slightly forwards, still in promenade position.
Slow	7	RIGHT FOOT takes a step forwards and across the left foot, still in promenade position.	7	LEFT FOOT takes a step forwards and across the right foot still in promenade position.
Quick	8	LEFT FOOT takes a step to the side, commencing to guide the lady to face you again.	8	RIGHT FOOT takes a step to the side, but starting to turn to face the man again.
Quick	9	RIGHT FOOT closes to left foot, keeping pressure on tips of right fingers to guide partner into normal hold.	9	LEFT FOOT closes to right foot, completing turn towards the man to regain normal hold.

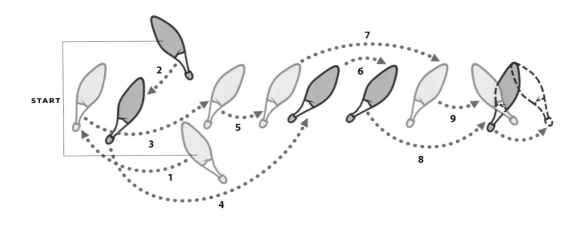

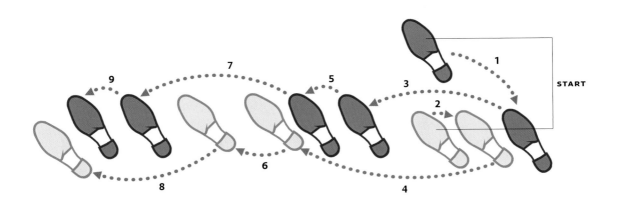

The Right Box with Right Turn

Slow

Slow

Quick

P **M** LEFT FOOT takes a small step to the side.
L RIGHT FOOT takes a small step to the side.

1 **M** RIGHT FOOT takes a step forwards.
L LEFT FOOT takes a step backwards.

2 **M** LEFT FOOT takes a small step to the side onto the same line as right foot.
L RIGHT FOOT takes a step to the side on the same line as left foot.

Slow

Quick

Quick

Slow

3 **M** RIGHT FOOT forwards and across your left foot.
L LEFT FOOT forwards and across your right foot. Both man and lady in promenade position.

4 **M** LEFT FOOT to the side and slightly forwards.
L RIGHT FOOT to the side and slightly forwards. Both man and lady in promenade position.

5 **M** RIGHT FOOT closes to left foot.
L LEFT FOOT closes to right foot. Both man and lady in promenade position.

6 **M** LEFT FOOT to the side and slightly forwards.
L RIGHT FOOT to the side and slightly forwards. Both man and lady in promenade position.

The Conversation Piece

Quick

Slow

Quick

Quick

3 **M** RIGHT FOOT closes to left foot, transferring weight onto right foot.
L LEFT FOOT closes to right foot, transferring weight onto left foot.

4 **M** LEFT FOOT takes a step backwards.
L RIGHT FOOT takes a step forwards.

1 **M** RIGHT FOOT takes a step to the side, guiding partner to turn right.
L LEFT FOOT takes a step to the side, turning to the right away from the man's left side.

2 **M** LEFT FOOT closes to right foot, still turning partner to the right.
L RIGHT FOOT closes to left foot, still turning towards the right into promenade position.

Slow

Quick

Quick

7 **M** RIGHT FOOT forwards and across left foot.
L LEFT FOOT forwards and across right foot. Both man and lady in promenade position.

8 **M** LEFT FOOT to the side, guiding the lady to face you again.
L RIGHT FOOT to the side, turning to face the man again.

9 **M** RIGHT FOOT closes to left foot, guiding partner into normal hold.
L LEFT FOOT closes to right foot, completing turn towards the man to regain normal hold.

Waltz

Waltzing couples at the Opera Ball in Vienna, Austria. This event takes places annually.

The Waltz has probably been around the longest out of any other current dance. It may not be the most popular, but it has seen off many dances that were temporarily more so.

DANCING to the GRAMOPHONE

By Appointment to H.M. the QUEEN.

ALL THE MOST
By FAMOUS BANDS and

POPULAR WALTZES
CELEBRATED ORCHESTRAS

THE GRAMOPHONE
is the only instrument recognised by the Greatest Artistes, and enables you to hear them to perfection in your own home.

THE GRAMOPHONE
is the Instrument chosen by the World's Greatest Artistes for the purpose of handing down to posterity the Living Voices of To-day and Yesterday.

Mme. MELBA writes:
"I am delighted with my latest Records. Your wonderful Gramophone improves year by year."

Signor CARUSO writes:
"I am indeed satisfied with my new Records. They are magnificent, and I congratulate you on the great improvement you have made in the last year."

Mme. PATTI writes:
"I am quite satisfied that future generations should hear my voice by means of the Gramophone, and I think the Record are faithful reproductions of my voice."

There are many kinds of Talking Machines, there is only one Gramophone.

Genuine Gramophone Needles
are sold only in metal boxes bearing our Trade Mark Picture, "His Master's Voice." It is most important that Gramophone Records should only be played with genuine Gramophone Needles.

On Receipt of Postcard
we will send Catalogue and Lists, also our Brochures, "Opera at Home" and "The Living Voice," together with Name and Address of the nearest Dealer in our Goods.

TRADE MARK
GRAMOPHONE

The GRAMOPHONE & TYPEWRITER, Ltd.
21 CITY ROAD, LONDON, E.C.

A magazine advertisement for the gramophone (c.1920s), which would allow you to listen and dance to popular waltzes by famous bands and orchestras.

The Waltz has a long history in Europe and has been taken up all over the world. It developed from peasant dances of the 16th and 17th centuries. Many authorities regard the Ländler and then the Weller as the roots of the modern dance in 3/4 time, that is, three beats to the bar of music. Both dances were popular in Austria and southern Germany, and danced to music in 3/4 time. Moreover, they were dances in which couples turned a great deal.

THE CLOSE HOLD Waltzes are danced in close hold (see page 18). This hold was first seen in England in the Elizabethan era in a dance called the Volta (see page 10). There is a famous painting at Penshurst Palace, Kent said to be of Queen Elizabeth I dancing it with the Earl of Leicester. It is interesting to compare the modes of the period with those of the Victorian era when it was even felt appropriate to hide table legs with thick stockings. Writing about the Volta, a 16th century writer, Phillip Stubbes, said: 'For what clipping, what culling, what kissing and bussing, what smooching and slabbering one of another, what filthie groping and uncleane handling is not practised in those dancings.'

When we now speak of waltzes we are talking about several versions. One, the so-called Viennese Waltz, is danced to fast music at a tempo of just under 60 bars per minute and is simple in its construction but more difficult in execution. To see a dance floor full of people flowing around the room dancing the Viennese Waltz is a wonderful, heady sight. Another version danced at a tempo of a little over 40 bars per minute is the Old Time Waltz. This dance, based on the five foot positions of ballet, was the popular Waltz in Britain up to World War I. It is still danced in Old Time Dance Clubs and forms the basis of many sequence dances.

At the end of the 19th and beginning of the 20th centuries an American version of waltzing, called the Boston, was popular with the dancing public. In this the couple stood facing in opposite directions but hip to hip. Originally it was taken at about 36–38 bars per

Carol Vorderman and Paul Killick dancing the Waltz in the second series of BBC TV's *Strictly Come Dancing*.

minute, but then succumbed to being a slow dance. In the current version the music tempo has dropped to 30 bars per minute and this is the one you will see in ballroom dancing competitions. In Britain, the popularity of this slow Waltz was first established in the mid-1920s when a particular version, called the Diagonal Waltz, proved successful in the World's Ballroom Dancing Championships.

For evidence of the permanence of the Waltz, look at the change in the dances used in the World's

In earlier days when modern light footwear was not available and floors were crude by comparison with modern dance floors, it is unlikely that our modern gliding dances could have been developed.

Ballroom Dancing Championships over the years. The first Championships after World War I in 1919 comprised the Waltz, the Tango, the Maxixe, the One-Step and the Foxtrot. In the following year the Spanish Schottische and the Shimmy were added to the above five dances.

The Waltz and the Tango are the only dances still with us. Today's Slow Foxtrot is not the same dance as the Foxtrot of the championships at that time. It was more related to our modern Quickstep. One other aspect of the development of our social dances relates to the improvement in footwear and the quality of our floors. In earlier days when modern light footwear was not available and floors were crude by comparison with modern maple or other dance floors, it is unlikely that our modern gliding dances could have been developed.

As in all aspects of life, change is inevitable and competition drives this on. Anyone who has seen ballroom dancing at the highest level will realize that the range of advanced figures used are not those likely to be used in social dancing. An art form has grown up that is as attractive to watch as any other form of dance. Many who start dancing purely socially will find themselves caught by the bug and progress a great deal further to higher or more sophisticated levels. The slow version of the Waltz is taught here and it is worth noting that British dancers have been pre-eminent in quite beautiful developments in the dance. For instance, Marcus and Karen Hilton (both of whom were awarded an MBE) recently retired from competitive dancing having won the World Professional Ballroom

Championships an unrivalled nine times. Another British couple Harry and Doreen Smith-Hampshire were acknowledged as pre-eminent in the rather specialized sphere of the Viennese Waltz.

However, this book is an introduction to dance, aimed at inexperienced dancers. The main objective is to encourage you to get onto the dance floor so that you too can enjoy social dancing. If you decide to go further and visit your local school of dance to widen your horizons then so much the better. So, on to the basic Waltz figures.

BASIC WALTZ FIGURES This dance is one of the so-called 'moving' dances and adopts the close hold throughout, maintaining body contact. The steps are fairly long compared with those of non-moving dances such as the Rumba. All steps forwards should be rather like walking but the foot should skim the floor when moving to position. It is a good idea to think that the foot is caressing the floor. Sideways steps will be taken on the ball of the foot or the toes. When stepping backwards you should try to straighten the ankle so that anyone standing behind you will see the sole of your shoe. As the weight of the body moves back onto the foot this rear foot acts like a spring to help control the weight changes and the balance.

The dance is in 3/4 time and this means three beats to the bar of music. On most simple figures you will take a step on each beat in the bar.

When the Waltz was first danced in Britain, Lord Byron, the poet, thought it immoral and wrote of it as looking like 'two cockchafers spitted on the same Bodekin'. Times have moved on!

Natasha Kaplinsky and Brendan Cole, winners of the first series of BBC TV's *Strictly Come Dancing*.

Left and Right Changes

In this group, also known as Change Steps, the side steps (following movements forwards) will, as a result of the body flow, be slightly forwards of the line set by the supporting foot and, similarly, side steps (following movements backwards) will be slightly backwards of the line. Forwards and backwards steps are walking type steps. When moving forwards they are taken on the heel. All side and closing steps should be taken on the ball of the foot or the toes. In the Waltz each step takes one beat of music, unless specified otherwise.

Man's Steps

Start with your right shoulder pointing to the nearest wall. You will be facing down the room in the direction dancers call 'facing line of dance'.

Lady's Steps

Start with your left shoulder pointing to the nearest wall. You will be backing down the room in the direction dancers call 'backing line of dance'.

Count:		**M**		**L**
One	1	LEFT FOOT takes a step forwards.	1	RIGHT FOOT takes a step backwards.
Two	2	RIGHT FOOT takes a step to the side on the same line as the left foot.	2	LEFT FOOT takes a step to the side on the same line as right foot.
Three	3	LEFT FOOT closes to right foot, taking care to place weight onto left foot, (beginners sometimes don't do so).	3	RIGHT FOOT closes to left foot taking care to place weight onto right foot, (beginners sometimes don't do so).
One	4	RIGHT FOOT takes a step forwards.	4	LEFT FOOT takes a step backwards.
Two	5	LEFT FOOT takes a step to the side on the same line as right foot.	5	RIGHT FOOT takes a step to the side on the same line as the left foot.
Three	6	RIGHT FOOT closes to left foot taking care to place weight onto right foot, (beginners sometimes don't do so).	6	LEFT FOOT closes to right foot taking care to place weight onto left foot, (beginners sometimes don't do so).

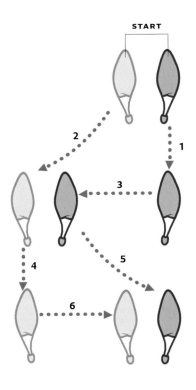

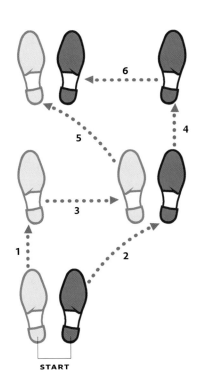

Left or Reverse Turn

When you feel comfortable with the Left and Right Changes (see pages 54–5), add a little variety by introducing the Left or Reverse Turn.

Man's Steps

Stand with right shoulder pointing to the nearest wall and turn about 45 degrees to left so that you are facing slanting into the room. This commencing position is called 'facing diagonally to centre'.

Lady's Steps

Stand with left shoulder pointing to the nearest wall and slightly turn to the left so that you are facing the wall in a slanting position. This commencing position is called 'backing diagonally to centre'.

Count:		M		L
One	1	LEFT FOOT takes a step forwards, beginning to turn to left.	1	RIGHT FOOT takes a step backwards, beginning to turn to left.
Two	2	RIGHT FOOT takes a step to the side, still turning left.	2	LEFT FOOT takes a step to the side, still turning to the left.
Three	3	LEFT FOOT closes to right foot still turning to left, the left shoulder should now be pointing towards the nearest wall.	3	RIGHT FOOT closes to left foot, still turning to left, the right shoulder should be pointing towards the nearest wall.
One	4	RIGHT FOOT takes a step backwards, still turning to the left.	4	LEFT FOOT takes a step forwards, still turning to left.
Two	5	LEFT FOOT takes a step to the side, still turning to the left.	5	RIGHT FOOT takes a step to the side, still turning to the left.
Three	6	RIGHT FOOT closes to left foot, completing the turn to the left, you should now be 'facing diagonally to wall'. Over the entire figure you should have made three-quarters of a full turn, for the mathematically inclined, 270 degrees.	6	LEFT FOOT closes to right foot, completing the turn to the left, you should now be 'backing diagonally to wall'. Over the entire figure you should have made three-quarters of a full turn, for the mathematically inclined, 270 degrees.

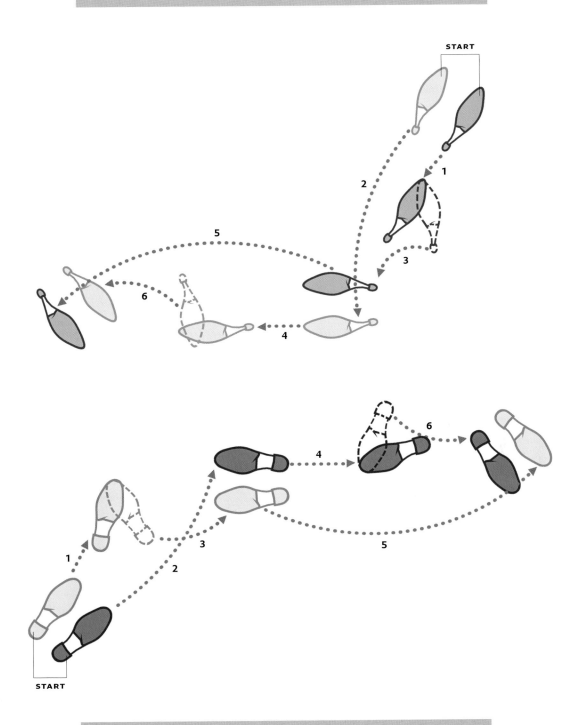

START

1

2

3

4

5

6

START

1

2

3

4

5

6

Left and Right Changes

One

Two

Three

1 **M** LEFT FOOT takes a step forwards.
L RIGHT FOOT takes a step backwards.

2 **M** RIGHT FOOT takes a step to the side on the same line as the left foot.
L LEFT FOOT takes a step to the side on same line as right foot.

3 **M** LEFT FOOT closes to right foot, taking weight onto left foot.
L RIGHT FOOT closes to left foot, taking weight onto right foot.

Left or Reverse Turn

One

Two

Three

1 **M** LEFT FOOT takes a step forwards, beginning to turn to left.
L RIGHT FOOT takes a step backwards, beginning to turn to left.

2 **M** RIGHT FOOT takes a step to the side, still turning to the left.
L LEFT FOOT takes a step to the side, still turning to the left.

3 **M** LEFT FOOT closes to right foot, still turning to the left.
L RIGHT FOOT closes to left foot, still turning to the left.

One

4 **M** RIGHT FOOT takes a step forwards.
L LEFT FOOT takes a step backwards.

Two

5 **M** LEFT FOOT to side on same line as right foot.
L RIGHT FOOT to side on the same line as left foot.

Three

6 **M** RIGHT FOOT closes to left foot, taking weight onto right foot.
L LEFT FOOT closes to right foot, taking weight onto left foot.

One

4 **M** RIGHT FOOT takes a step backwards, still turning to the left.
L LEFT FOOT takes a step forwards, still turning to the left.

Two

5 **M** LEFT FOOT takes a step to the side, still turning to the left.
L RIGHT FOOT takes a step to the side, still turning to the left.

Three

6 **M** RIGHT FOOT closes to left foot, completing the turn to the left.
L LEFT FOOT closes to right foot, completing the turn to the left.

Right or Natural Turn

This figure is preceded and followed by Left and Right Change Steps. It can also follow the Reverse Turn and that amalgamation of 18 steps can be repeated.

Man's Steps

Start by facing slanting out of the room in the forwards direction, referred to as 'facing diagonally to wall' by dancers.

Count:		**M**
One	1	LEFT FOOT takes a step forwards.
Two	2	RIGHT FOOT takes a step to the side on the same line as the left foot.
Three	3	LEFT FOOT closes to right foot.
One	4	RIGHT FOOT takes a step forwards, beginning to turn to the right.
Two	5	LEFT FOOT takes a step to the side, still turning to the right.
Three	6	RIGHT FOOT closes to left foot still turning to the right. Your left shoulder should now be pointing towards the nearest wall.

Count:		
One	7	LEFT FOOT takes a step backwards, still turning to the right.
Two	8	RIGHT FOOT takes a step to the side, still turning to the right.
Three	9	LEFT FOOT closes to right foot, completing the turn to the right. You should now be 'facing diagonally to centre'.
One	10	RIGHT FOOT takes a step forwards.
Two	11	LEFT FOOT takes a step to the side on the same line as right foot.
Three	12	RIGHT FOOT closes to left foot, 'facing diagonally to centre'.

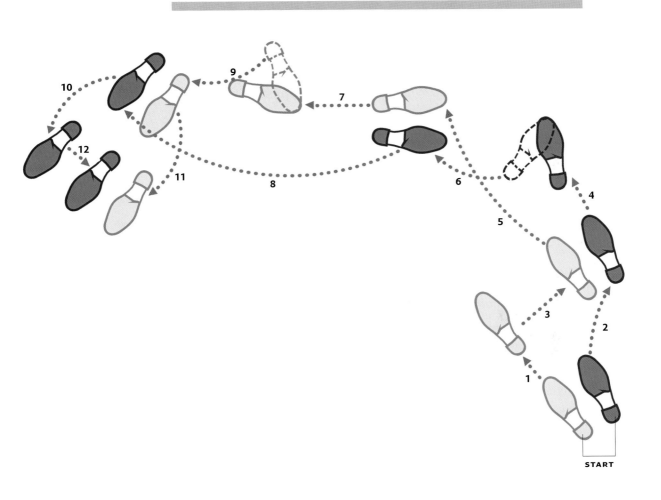

Right or Natural Turn

Lady's Steps

Start by backing slightly out of the room in a backwards direction, referred to as 'backing diagonally to wall' by dancers.

Count: **L**

One	1	RIGHT FOOT takes a step backwards.
Two	2	LEFT FOOT takes a step to side on the same line as the right foot.
Three	3	RIGHT FOOT closes to left foot.
One	4	LEFT FOOT takes a step backwards, beginning to turn to the right.
Two	5	RIGHT FOOT takes a step to the side, still turning to the right.
Three	6	LEFT FOOT closes to right foot still turning to right. Your right shoulder should now be pointing towards the nearest wall.

Count:

One	7	RIGHT FOOT takes a step forwards, still turning to right.
Two	8	LEFT FOOT takes a step to the side, still turning to the right.
Three	9	RIGHT FOOT closes to left foot, completing the turn to the right. You should now be 'backing diagonally to centre'.
One	10	LEFT FOOT takes a step backwards.
Two	11	RIGHT FOOT takes a step to the side on the same line as left foot.
Three	12	LEFT FOOT closes to right foot, 'backing diagonally to centre'.

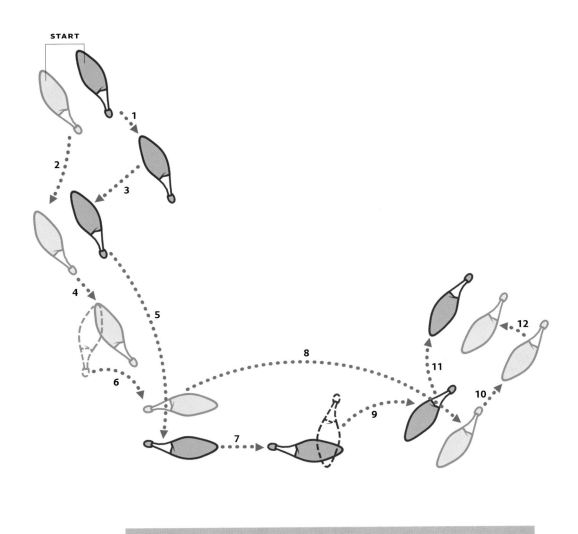

START

Right or Natural Turn

One

1 **M** LEFT FOOT takes a step forwards.
L RIGHT FOOT takes a step backwards.

Two

2 **M** RIGHT FOOT takes a step to the side on the same line as the left foot.
L LEFT FOOT takes a step to the side on the same line as the right foot.

Three

3 **M** LEFT FOOT closes to right foot.
L RIGHT FOOT closes to left foot.

One

7 **M** LEFT FOOT takes a step backwards, still turning to the right.
L RIGHT FOOT takes a step forwards, still turning to the right.

Two

8 **M** RIGHT FOOT takes a step to the side, still turning to the right.
L LEFT FOOT takes a step to the side, still turning to the right.

Three

9 **M** LEFT FOOT closes to right foot, completing the turn to the right.
L RIGHT FOOT closes to left foot, completing the turn to the right.

One	Two	Three

4 **M** RIGHT FOOT takes a step forwards, beginning to turn to right.
L LEFT FOOT takes a step backwards, beginning to turn to right.

5 **M** LEFT FOOT takes a step to the side, still turning to right.
L RIGHT FOOT takes a step to the side, still turning to right.

6 **M** RIGHT FOOT closes to left foot, still turning to the right.
L LEFT FOOT closes to right foot, still turning to the right.

One	Two	Three

10 **M** RIGHT FOOT takes a step forwards.
L LEFT FOOT takes a step backwards.

11 **M** LEFT FOOT takes a step to the side on same line as right foot.
L RIGHT FOOT takes a step to the side on same line as left foot.

12 **M** RIGHT FOOT closes to left foot.
L LEFT FOOT closes to right foot.

The Whisk, Chassé and Right or Natural Turn

The Whisk is one of the most popular figures in all dances but it was first created in the Waltz in about 1930. The Chassé that follows introduces a syncopated rhythm where two steps are taken in the time of one beat. Also, for the first time in the Waltz, stepping 'outside partner' is introduced, whereby a step is taken to one side of your partner. This grouping can follow the Left or Reverse Turn.

Man's Steps

Start by 'facing diagonally to wall'.

Count:		M
One	1	LEFT FOOT takes a step forwards, starting to increase pressure of the heel of your right hand on lady's back.
Two	2	RIGHT FOOT takes a step to the side, turning partner so that she turns her right side away from your left side, you do not turn. The lead should come from your right hand.
Three	3	LEFT FOOT crosses loosely behind right foot, continuing to lead the lady to complete her turn, so that she finishes with her right side roughly 30 cm (11 ¾ in) away from your hip in promenade position.
One	4	RIGHT FOOT takes a step forwards and across left foot along a line parallel with the nearest wall, still in promenade position.
Two	5	LEFT FOOT takes a step to the side along the line parallel with the wall, starting to increase pressure of fingers of right hand on the lady's back, taking only half a beat of music.

Count:		
And	6	RIGHT FOOT closes to left foot, continuing to press on lady's back with right finger tips to bring her back to face you, taking half a beat of music.
Three	7	LEFT FOOT takes a step to the side, still moving along a line parallel with nearest wall. The lady should now be facing you.
One	8	RIGHT FOOT takes a step forwards to your left of your partner's feet, 'outside partner', starting to turn to the right.
Two	9	LEFT FOOT takes a step to the side, still turning right, and as this step is taken your partner comes into line with you again.
Three	10	RIGHT FOOT closes to left foot, still turning right, your left shoulder should be pointing towards the nearest wall, that is, 'backing line of dance'.
One	11	LEFT FOOT takes a step backwards, still turning to the right.
Two	12	RIGHT FOOT takes a step to the side, still turning to the right.
Three	13	LEFT FOOT closes to right foot, completing the turn to the right, you should now be 'facing diagonally to centre'.

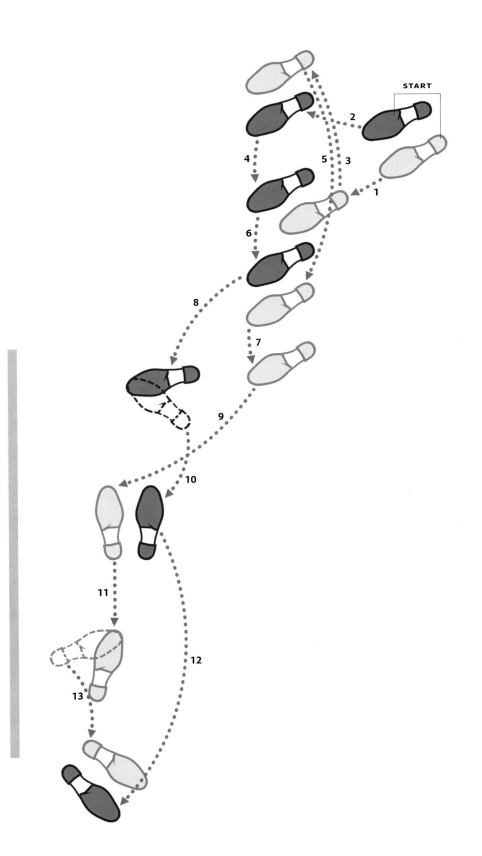

START

The Whisk, Chassé and Right or Natural Turn

Lady's Steps

Start by 'backing diagonally to wall'.

Count:	L		Count:		
One	1	RIGHT FOOT takes a step backwards.	Three	7	RIGHT FOOT takes a step to the side, still moving along a line parallel with nearest wall.
Two	2	LEFT FOOT takes a step to the side, turning your right side away from man's left side.	One	8	LEFT FOOT takes a step backwards and your partner steps to the right of your feet, 'outside partner', starting to turn to the right.
Three	3	RIGHT FOOT crosses loosely behind left foot, continuing to turn so that you finish with your right side roughly 30 cm (11 ¾ in) away from your partner's hip in promenade position.	Two	9	RIGHT FOOT takes a step to the side, still turning right, and as this step is taken your partner comes into line with you again.
One	4	LEFT FOOT takes a step forwards and across right foot along a line parallel with the nearest wall, commencing to turn to left, still in promenade position.	Three	10	LEFT FOOT closes to right foot, still turning, your right shoulder should be pointing towards the nearest wall, that is, 'facing line of dance'.
Two	5	RIGHT FOOT takes a step to the side along the line parallel with the wall, still turning to the left, taking half a beat of music.	One	11	RIGHT FOOT takes a step forwards, still turning to the right.
			Two	12	LEFT FOOT takes a step to the side, still turning to the right.
And	6	LEFT FOOT closes to right foot, continuing to turn to the left, you should now be facing the man, taking half a beat of music.	Three	13	RIGHT FOOT closes to left foot still turning to the right, you should now be 'backing diagonally to centre'.

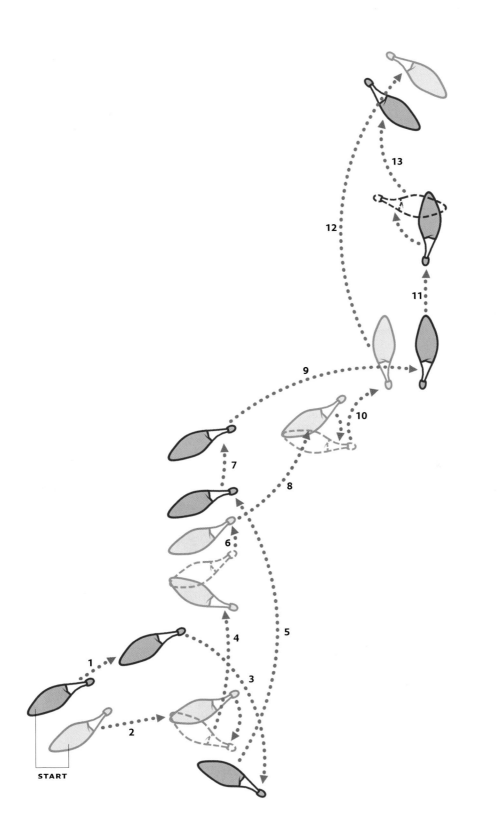

START

The Whisk

One

Two

Three

1 **M** LEFT FOOT takes a step forwards, starting to increase pressure of the heel of right hand on lady's back.
L RIGHT FOOT takes a step backwards.

2 **M** RIGHT FOOT takes a step to the side, turning your partner with right hand.
L LEFT FOOT takes a step to the side, turning right side away from man's left side.

3 **M** LEFT FOOT crosses loosely behind right foot, still leading the lady.
L RIGHT FOOT crosses loosely behind left foot, still turning to promenade position.

Right or Natural Turn

One

Two

Three

One

8 **M** RIGHT FOOT steps forwards to your left of partner's feet, 'outside partner', turning to right.
L LEFT FOOT steps backwards starting to turn to right.

9 **M** LEFT FOOT takes a step to the side, still turning to right, partner comes into line with you again.
L RIGHT FOOT takes a step to the side, still turning to right.

10 **M** RIGHT FOOT closes to left foot, still turning to the right and 'backing line of dance'.
L LEFT FOOT closes to right foot, turning right and 'facing line of dance'.

11 **M** LEFT FOOT takes a step backwards, still turning to the right.
L RIGHT FOOT takes a step forwards, still turning to the right.

Chassé

One

Two

And

Three

4 **M** RIGHT FOOT forwards and across left foot, parallel with the wall.
L LEFT FOOT forwards and across right foot, parallel with the wall, starting to turn to left.

5 **M** LEFT FOOT steps to the side, parallel with the wall.
L RIGHT FOOT steps to the side, parallel with the wall, still turning to left. Takes half a beat of music.

6 **M** RIGHT FOOT closes to left foot, continuing to press on lady's back.
L LEFT FOOT closes to right foot, still turning to to the left. You should now be facing the man.

7 **M** LEFT FOOT takes a step to the side, along a line parallel with the wall.
L RIGHT FOOT takes a step to the side, still moving along a line parallel with the wall.

Two

Three

12 **M** RIGHT FOOT takes a step to the side, still turning to the right.
L LEFT FOOT takes a step to the side, still turning to the right.

13 **M** LEFT FOOT closes to right foot, completing the turn to the right.
L RIGHT FOOT closes to left foot, completing the turn to the right.

To see a dance floor full of people flowing around the room dancing the Viennese Waltz is a wonderful, heady sight.

Cha Cha Cha

Julian Clary and Erin Boag perform the Cha Cha Cha as their first dance on BBC TV's *Strictly Come Dancing*.

Cuban music and dance has had an enormous impact on dancing throughout the world, to such an extent that three of the dances in this book – Salsa, Rumba and Cha Cha Cha – are Cuban in origin.

For several years Cha Cha Cha has been the most popular of the Latin American dances, although Salsa has probably now overtaken it. Like Salsa, the Cha Cha Cha has Cuban roots, however, the dance has also been heavily influenced by the American music scene.

As in all dances, response to the music is vital, and you should try and get some good Cuban recordings and note the repeated patterns of the rhythm. In Cha Cha Cha you should listen out for the triplet of beats that occurs around the end of each bar of music. It is quick and the sound 'de de dah' is what you should be listening for.

Whenever you hear the 'de de dah' rhythmic break, you should be fitting three steps to that rhythm. These are the basis of the Cha Cha Chah. (Note the last beat is Chah with an 'h.')

THE HOLD In this dance the man and lady do not stand in body contact with each other but use the Open Hold (see page 18).

All figures in the Cha Cha Cha do not move around the room and can be commenced facing in any direction. However, to start with, the man should try facing the nearest wall and the lady should face him. Basic footwork involves stepping on the ball of your foot first, then lowering the rest of your foot.

The Cha Cha Cha came to prominence in the 1950s. Here Brigitte Bardot does the dance under the direction of comedian, Darius Moreno, in the 1959 French film *Voulez-Vous Danser Avec Moi?*

Members of the Arthur Murray Dance School (above) doing the Cha Cha Cha. Arthur Murray established himself in the 1930s with a dance correspondence course, featuring his 'Magic Step'.

Starter Pattern

Some beginners find the rhythm a little tricky and it will help to put you on the correct beat if you always begin with the following Cha Cha Cha starter pattern, which includes a preparatory step taken on the first beat of the bar of music.

Count:		**Man's Steps**
	P	LEFT FOOT marks time in place, taking one beat of music.
Step	1	RIGHT FOOT marks time in place, taking one beat of music.
Step	2	LEFT FOOT marks time in place, taking one beat of music.
Cha	3	RIGHT FOOT takes a small step to the side, taking half a beat of music.
Cha	4	LEFT FOOT closes towards right foot, taking half a beat of music.
Chah	5	RIGHT FOOT takes a small step to the side, taking one beat of music.

Count:		**Lady's Steps**
	P	RIGHT FOOT marks time in place, taking one beat of music.
Step	1	LEFT FOOT marks time in place, taking one beat of music.
Step	2	RIGHT FOOT marks time in place, taking one beat of music.
Cha	3	LEFT FOOT takes a small step to the side, taking half a beat of music.
Cha	4	RIGHT FOOT closes towards left foot, taking half a beat of music.
Chah	5	LEFT FOOT takes a small step to the side, taking one beat of music.

Forwards and Backwards Cha Cha Cha Basics

This figure can follow the Starter Pattern on page 75.

	Man's Steps		Lady's Steps

Count:	**M**		**L**

Step	**1**	LEFT FOOT takes a step forwards, taking one beat of music.	**1**	RIGHT FOOT takes a step backwards, taking one beat of music.
Step	**2**	RIGHT FOOT remains in place with the weight taken back onto it, taking one beat of music.	**2**	LEFT FOOT remains in place with the weight taken forwards onto it, taking one beat of music.
Cha	**3**	LEFT FOOT takes a step to the side, taking half a beat of music.	**3**	RIGHT FOOT takes a step to the side, taking half a beat of music.
Cha	**4**	RIGHT FOOT closes towards but not up to left foot, taking half a beat of music.	**4**	LEFT FOOT closes towards but not up to right foot, taking half a beat of music.
Chah	**5**	LEFT FOOT takes a step to the side, taking one beat of music.	**5**	RIGHT FOOT takes a step to the side, taking one beat of music.
Step	**6**	RIGHT FOOT takes a step backwards, taking one beat of music.	**6**	LEFT FOOT takes a step forwards, taking one beat of music.
Step	**7**	LEFT FOOT remains in place with the weight taken forwards onto it, taking one beat of music.	**7**	RIGHT FOOT remains in place with the weight taken back onto it, taking one beat of music.
Cha	**8**	RIGHT FOOT takes a step to the side, taking half a beat of music.	**8**	LEFT FOOT takes a step to the side, taking half a beat of music.
Cha	**9**	LEFT FOOT closes towards but not up to right foot, taking half a beat of music.	**9**	RIGHT FOOT closes towards but not up to left foot, taking half a beat of music.
Chah	**10**	RIGHT FOOT takes a small step to the side, taking one beat of music.	**10**	LEFT FOOT takes a step to the side, taking one beat of music.

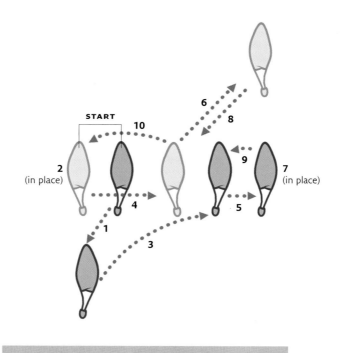

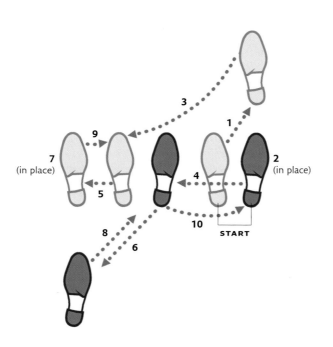

Forwards and Backwards Cha Cha Cha Basics

Step

1 **M** LEFT FOOT takes a step forwards.
L RIGHT FOOT takes a step backwards.
Takes one beat of music.

Step

2 **M** RIGHT FOOT remains in place with the weight back onto it.
L LEFT FOOT remains in place with the weight taken forwards onto it.
Takes one beat of music.

Step

6 **M** RIGHT FOOT takes a step backwards.
L LEFT FOOT takes a step forwards.
Takes one beat of music.

Step

7 **M** LEFT FOOT remains in place with the weight taken forwards onto it.
L RIGHT FOOT remains in place with the weight back onto it.
Takes one beat of music.

Cha

8 **M** RIGHT FOOT takes a step to the side.
L LEFT FOOT takes a step to the side.
Takes half a beat of music.

Cha

Cha

Chah

3 **M** LEFT FOOT takes a step
to the side.
L RIGHT FOOT takes a step
to the side.
Takes half a beat of
music.

4 **M** RIGHT FOOT closes
towards left foot.
L LEFT FOOT closes
towards right foot.
Takes half a beat
of music.

5 **M** LEFT FOOT takes a step
to the side.
L RIGHT FOOT takes a step
to the side.
Takes one beat of music.

Cha

Chah

9 **M** LEFT FOOT closes
towards right foot.
L RIGHT FOOT closes
towards left foot.
Takes half a beat of
music.

10 **M** RIGHT FOOT takes a step
to the side.
L LEFT FOOT takes a step
to the side.
Takes one beat of music.

In Place Basic Cha Cha Chas

This figure is also known as Time Steps. The man and the lady should start with their feet slightly apart.

		Man's Steps			Lady's Steps
Count:		**M**			**L**
Step	1	LEFT FOOT closes to right foot.	1		RIGHT FOOT closes to left foot.
Step	2	RIGHT FOOT marks time in place.	2		LEFT FOOT marks time in place.
Cha	3	LEFT FOOT takes a small step to the side, starting the cha cha cha rhythm break leftwards, that is, moving in the opposite direction to the preceding step.	3		RIGHT FOOT takes a small step to the side, starting the cha cha cha rhythm break rightwards, that is, moving in the opposite direction to the preceding step.
Cha	4	RIGHT FOOT closes towards but not up to left foot.	4		LEFT FOOT closes towards but not up to right foot.
Chah	5	LEFT FOOT takes a small step to the side.	5		RIGHT FOOT takes a small step to the side.
Step	6	RIGHT FOOT closes to left foot.	6		LEFT FOOT closes to right foot.
Step	7	LEFT FOOT marks time in place.	7		RIGHT FOOT marks time in place.
Cha	8	RIGHT FOOT takes a small step to the side, starting the cha cha cha rhythm break rightwards, that is, moving in the opposite direction to the preceding step.	8		LEFT FOOT takes a small step to the side, starting the cha cha cha rhythm break leftwards, that is, moving in opposite direction to preceding step.
Cha	9	LEFT FOOT closes towards but not up to right foot.	9		RIGHT FOOT closes towards but not up to left foot.
Chah	10	RIGHT FOOT takes a small step to the side.	10		LEFT FOOT takes a small step to the side.

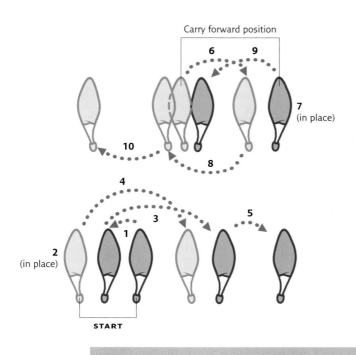

Carry forward position

6   9

7
(in place)

10

8

4

3

1

5

2
(in place)

START

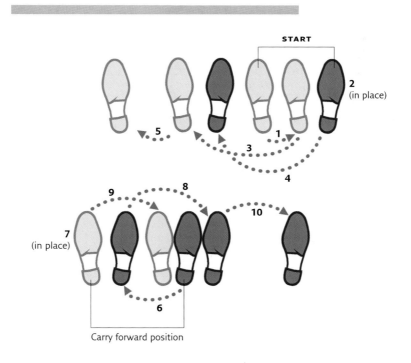

START

2
(in place)

5

3

1

4

9   8

10

7
(in place)

6

Carry forward position

In Place Basic Cha Cha Chas

Step

1 **M** LEFT FOOT closes to right foot.
L RIGHT FOOT closes to left foot.

Step

2 **M** RIGHT FOOT marks time in place.
L LEFT FOOT marks time in place.

Step

6 **M** RIGHT FOOT closes to left foot.
L LEFT FOOT closes to right foot.

Step

7 **M** LEFT FOOT marks time in place.
L RIGHT FOOT marks time in place.

Cha

8 **M** RIGHT FOOT to the side, starting the cha cha cha rhythm break rightwards.
L LEFT FOOT to the side, starting the cha cha cha rhythm break leftwards.

Cha

Cha

Chah

3 **M** LEFT FOOT to the side, starting the cha cha cha rhythm break leftwards.
L RIGHT FOOT to the side, starting the cha cha cha rhythm break rightwards.

4 **M** RIGHT FOOT closes towards but not up to left foot.
L LEFT FOOT closes towards but not up to right foot.

5 **M** LEFT FOOT takes a small step to the side.
L RIGHT FOOT takes a small step to the side.

Cha

Chah

9 **M** LEFT FOOT closes towards but not up to right foot.
L RIGHT FOOT closes towards but not up to left foot.

10 **M** RIGHT FOOT takes a small step to the side.
L LEFT FOOT takes a small step to the side.

The Fan

In the Fan, the man releases hold of the lady with his right hand, guides her to move to his left side and turn, so that she is facing at roughly right angles to him. Follow the steps below to reach the Fan position. This figure is usually followed by the Hockey Stick (see pages 88-91).

		Man's Steps		Lady's Steps
Count:		**M**		**L**
Step	1	LEFT FOOT takes a small step forwards.	1	RIGHT FOOT takes a small step backwards.
Step	2	RIGHT FOOT remains in place with the weight back onto it.	2	LEFT FOOT remains in place with the weight forwards onto it.
Cha	3	LEFT FOOT takes a step to the side, turning to the left.	3	RIGHT FOOT takes a step to the side turning to the left.
Cha	4	RIGHT FOOT closes towards but not up to left foot.	4	LEFT FOOT closes towards but not up to right foot.
Chah	5	LEFT FOOT takes a step to the side, turning to the left and lowering your left arm.	5	RIGHT FOOT takes a step to the side, turning to the right and lowering your right arm.
Step	6	RIGHT FOOT takes a step backwards, leading partner to step to the left of your feet, that is, 'outside partner'.	6	LEFT FOOT takes a step forwards to your right of both your partner's feet, that is, 'outside partner'.
Step	7	LEFT FOOT remains in place with the weight taken forwards onto it. Turn the lady to her left by pulling your left hand back and releasing hold of her with your right hand.	7	RIGHT FOOT takes a step forwards, then turn to the left on both feet to finish with your right foot backwards.
Cha	8	RIGHT FOOT takes a step to the side, turning to your left. The lady should almost be at right angles to you and stepping back away from you.	8	LEFT FOOT takes a step backwards, still turning to the left to finish at almost right angles to your partner.
Cha	9	LEFT FOOT closes towards right foot, still turning to your left.	9	RIGHT FOOT closes towards left foot, still turning to the left. At this point you can cross the right foot in front of the left foot.
Chah	10	RIGHT FOOT takes a small step to the side. You are now at right angles to your partner, holding her right hand in your left hand.	10	LEFT FOOT takes a small step backwards. You are now at right angles to your partner, he is holding your right hand in his left hand.

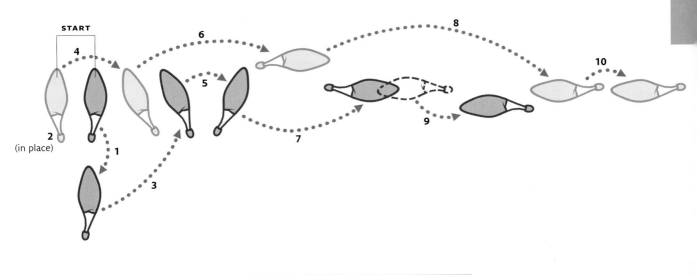

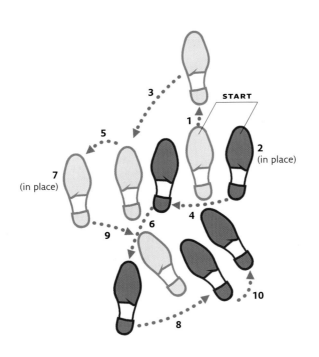

The Fan

1   **M** LEFT FOOT takes a small step forwards.
L RIGHT FOOT takes a small step backwards.

2   **M** RIGHT FOOT remains in place taking the weight back onto it.
L LEFT FOOT remains in place with the weight forwards onto it.

3   **M** LEFT FOOT takes a step to the side, turning to the left.
L RIGHT FOOT takes a step to the side turning to the left.

Step

Cha

7   **M** LEFT FOOT remains forwards in place. Turn lady to left, release hold of her with right hand.
L RIGHT FOOT forwards, then turn to left, end with right foot backwards.

8   **M** RIGHT FOOT takes a step to the side.
L LEFT FOOT takes a step backwards, still turning to the left, now almost at right angles to your partner.

Cha

Chah

Step

4 **M** RIGHT FOOT closes towards but not up to left foot.
L LEFT FOOT closes towards but not up to right foot.

5 **M** LEFT FOOT to the side, turning to the left and lowering left arm.
L RIGHT FOOT to the side, turning to the right and lowering right arm.

6 **M** RIGHT FOOT takes a step backwards, leading partner to step 'outside partner'.
L LEFT FOOT takes a step forwards, 'outside partner'.

Cha

Chah

9 **M** LEFT FOOT closes towards right foot.
L RIGHT FOOT closes towards left foot, still turning to the left. You can cross the right foot in front of the left foot.

10 **M** RIGHT FOOT takes a step to the side.
L LEFT FOOT takes a step backwards. You are now at right angles to your partner.

The Hockey Stick

In this figure, which follows the Fan (see pages 84–7), the man turns the lady to her left under his left and her right hands. Partners will end up facing each other, holding hands and at a short distance from one another in the open position.

		Man's Steps **M**		Lady's Steps **L**
Count:				
Step	1	LEFT FOOT takes a step forwards, do not pull on the lady's hand with your left hand as she has to remain in position.	1	RIGHT FOOT closes towards left foot.
Step	2	RIGHT FOOT remains in place with the weight back onto it, starting to bring your left hand forwards and across your body, guiding the lady forwards.	2	LEFT FOOT takes a step forwards, moving towards partner.
Cha	3	LEFT FOOT takes a step to the side, starting to raise your left hand.	3	RIGHT FOOT takes a step forwards.
Cha	4	RIGHT FOOT closes towards but not up to left foot, keeping your left hand raised.	4	LEFT FOOT closes towards right foot, or, if you are adventurous, loosely cross it behind your right foot.
Chah	5	LEFT FOOT takes a step to the side, passing your left and the lady's right hand over the lady's head, then lower your left hand onto her shoulder. Do not grip her hand tightly, she must be free to turn.	5	RIGHT FOOT takes a step forwards, moving your right hand over your head onto your left shoulder.
Step	6	RIGHT FOOT takes a step backwards, starting to turn a little to the right.	6	LEFT FOOT takes a step forwards, starting to turn left.
Step	7	LEFT FOOT remains in place with the weight forwards onto it, then lower your left hand to the normal position. By the end of the step the lady will be facing you.	7	RIGHT FOOT steps forwards, then turn to the left on both feet to finish with right foot backwards, facing partner.
Cha	8	RIGHT FOOT takes a step forwards towards partner.	8	LEFT FOOT takes a step backwards.
Cha	9	LEFT FOOT closes towards right foot.	9	RIGHT FOOT closes towards left foot.
Chah	10	RIGHT FOOT takes a step forwards.	10	LEFT FOOT takes a step backwards, facing your partner with your right hand in his left hand and with your left hand free.

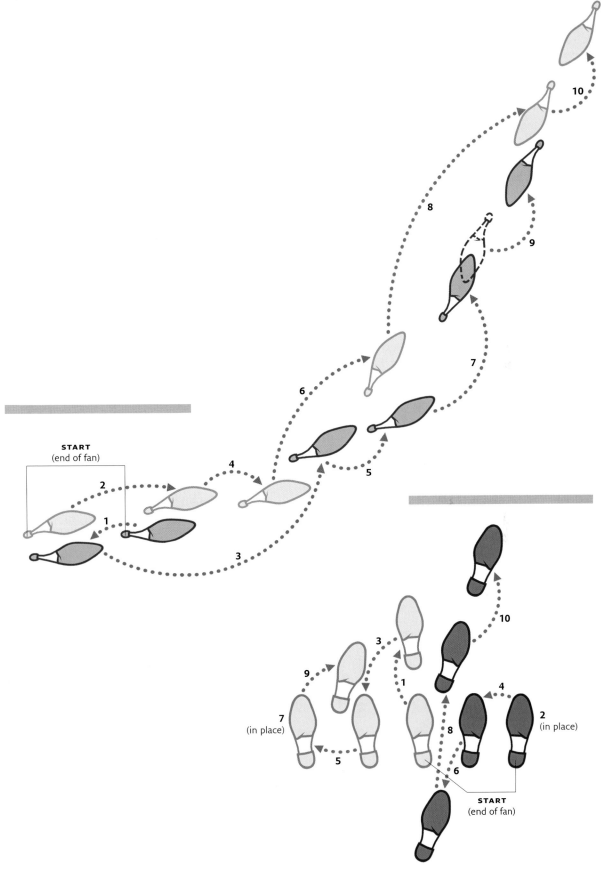

The Lock Step

In the Cha Cha Chah rhythmic break, forwards or backwards, advanced dancers use a lock step – step, cross, step. The first step is taken forwards, the second step crosses loosely behind, then the third step is taken forwards again. When moving backwards, the second step crosses loosely in front of the first step backwards. For example, a forwards lock step is:
1) Right foot forwards.
2) Left foot crosses loosely behind right foot.
3) Right foot forwards.

The Hockey Stick

Step

Step

1 **M** LEFT FOOT forwards, do not pull on the lady's hand as she has to remain in position.
L RIGHT FOOT closes towards left foot.

2 **M** RIGHT FOOT remains in place with weight back onto it, starting to guide the lady to step forwards.
L LEFT FOOT takes a step forwards, moving towards partner.

Step

Step

Cha

6 **M** RIGHT FOOT steps backwards, starting to turn a little to the right.
L LEFT FOOT steps forwards, starting to turn to the left.

7 **M** LEFT FOOT remains forwards in place, then lower left hand to normal position.
L RIGHT FOOT forwards, then turn to left to finish facing partner.

8 **M** RIGHT FOOT takes a step forwards towards partner.
L LEFT FOOT takes a step backwards.

Cha

Cha

Chah

3 **M** LEFT FOOT takes a step to the side, starting to raise your left hand.
  L RIGHT FOOT takes a step forwards.

4 **M** RIGHT FOOT closes towards left foot, keeping left hand raised.
  L LEFT FOOT closes towards right foot, you can loosely cross it behind your right foot.

5 **M** LEFT FOOT to the side, passing your left and lady's right hands over her head, lowering hands onto her left shoulder.
  L RIGHT FOOT takes a step forwards.

Cha

Chah

9 **M** LEFT FOOT closes towards right foot.
  L RIGHT FOOT closes towards left foot.

10 **M** RIGHT FOOT takes a step forwards.
  L LEFT FOOT takes a step backwards.

Back to Normal

At the end of the Hockey Stick, partners are still separated and have not returned to the normal hold. This is achieved by the man drawing the lady towards him while dancing the basic movement.

The Alemana

After the Fan, rather than the Hockey Stick, the Alemana can be danced. In this figure the lady turns to her right instead of her left. The instructions below are for the Alemana taken from the Fan position.

Man's Steps

The man does not turn in this figure.

Lady's Steps

In steps 5–10 imagine you are walking around a small plate, you will make one and a quarter turns to your right.

Count:		M		L
Step	1	LEFT FOOT takes a small step forwards, do not pull on the lady's hand with your left hand as she has to remain momentarily away from you.	1	RIGHT FOOT closes to left foot.
Step	2	RIGHT FOOT remains in place with the weight back onto it, starting to bring your left hand forwards and across your body, guiding partner forwards.	2	LEFT FOOT takes a step forwards moving towards partner.
Cha	3	LEFT FOOT takes a step to the side, starting to raise your left hand.	3	RIGHT FOOT takes a step forwards.
Cha	4	RIGHT FOOT closes towards but not up to left foot, keeping left hand raised.	4	LEFT FOOT closes towards right foot, and can cross loosely behind it.
Chah	5	LEFT FOOT takes a step to the side, starting to turn the lady strongly to her right by rotating the joined hands clockwise. Do not grip tightly.	5	RIGHT FOOT takes a step forwards, starting the strong turn to the right.
Step	6	RIGHT FOOT takes a step backwards, continuing to turn the lady to her right.	6	LEFT FOOT takes a step forwards, turning strongly to the right.
Step	7	LEFT FOOT remains in place with the weight forwards onto it, continuing to turn the lady to her right.	7	RIGHT FOOT takes a step forwards, still turning strongly to the right.
Cha	8	RIGHT FOOT takes a step to the side, with the lady still turning.	8	LEFT FOOT takes a step to the side, still turning to the right.
Cha	9	LEFT FOOT closes towards right foot, with the lady still turning.	9	RIGHT FOOT closes towards left foot, still turning to the right.
Chah	10	RIGHT FOOT takes a step to the side, you are now facing your partner. Regain normal hold.	10	LEFT FOOT takes a step to the side, you are now facing your partner. Regain normal hold.

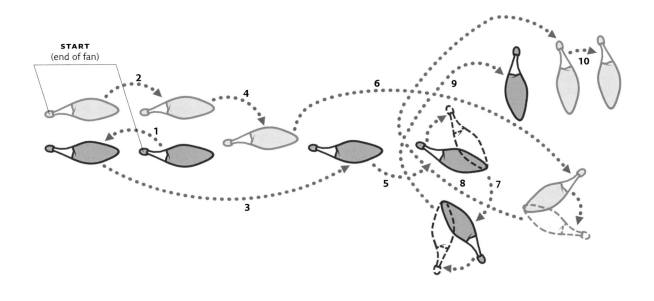

START
(end of fan)

1   2   3   4   5   6   7   8   9   10

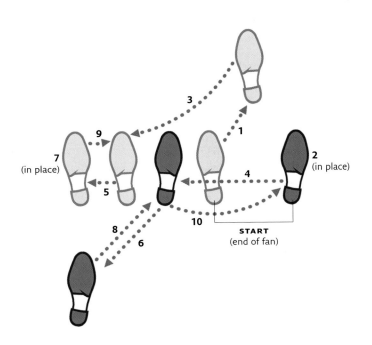

7
(in place)

2
(in place)

START
(end of fan)

The Alemana

1 **M** LEFT FOOT takes a step forwards, do not pull on the lady's hand, she has to remain in position.
L RIGHT FOOT closes to left foot.

2 **M** RIGHT FOOT remains in place with weight back onto it, while left hand guides partner forwards.
L LEFT FOOT takes a step forwards, moving towards partner.

Step

Step

Cha

6 **M** RIGHT FOOT takes a step backwards, still turning partner to her right.
L LEFT FOOT takes a step forwards, turning strongly to the right.

7 **M** LEFT FOOT remains in place with the weight forwards onto it, still turning lady to her right.
L RIGHT FOOT takes a step forwards, still turning strongly to the right.

8 **M** RIGHT FOOT takes a step to the side, lady still turning.
L LEFT FOOT takes a step to the side, still turning to the right.

Cha

3 **M** LEFT FOOT takes a step
to the side, starting to
raise your left hand.
L RIGHT FOOT takes a step
forwards.

Cha

4 **M** RIGHT FOOT closes
towards but not up to
left foot, keeping your
left hand raised.
L LEFT FOOT closes
towards right foot and
may cross behind it.

Chah

5 **M** LEFT FOOT takes a step
to the side, starting to
turn the lady strongly to
her right.
L RIGHT FOOT takes a step
forwards, starting the
strong turn to the right.

Cha

9 **M** LEFT FOOT closes
towards right foot, with
the lady still turning.
L RIGHT FOOT closes
towards left foot, still
turning to the right.

Chah

10 **M** RIGHT FOOT takes a step
to the side to face your
partner.
L LEFT FOOT takes a step
to the side to face your
partner.
Regain normal hold .

Quickstep

The intricate footwork and elaborate costumes of
an experienced ballroom dancing couple.

The Quickstep is a British dance that developed from American dances in the post-World War I years. It is a development from the Foxtrot that came to the fore in the USA in 1914. The Foxtrot can, in turn, possibly be traced to the One Step and Castle Walk of the years immediately preceding the War.

Diarmuid Gavin and Nicole Cutler's rendition of the Quickstep for BBC TV's *Strictly Come Dancing*.

The Castle Walk was named after Irene and Vernon Castle, who made an immense reputation as dancers in the years pre-World War I. Vernon Castle was British, born in Norwich as Vernon Blyth, before he adopted the name Castle. He emigrated to the USA where he married Irene. When War broke out, he returned to England to volunteer for the Royal Air Force. Sadly he was killed in an air crash.

In Britain, the Castle Walk developed into two versions, one quick and one slow. In due course, following modifications, one has become our Quickstep and the other the Slow Foxtrot. The latter is a particularly British development, although it did have some American input. The basis of the modern Slow Foxtrot was laid in the early 1920s and prominent in its development and promotion were Britain's Queen of the Ballroom, Josephine Bradley, and Mr G. K. Anderson, who was an American amateur dancer.

FAST VERSION The early version of a fast Foxtrot was known, in Britain, as the Quick-Time Foxtrot and Charleston, but in a short space of time it became known as the Quickstep. In the USA, a very fast version of the Foxtrot became known as the Peabody or the Roseland Foxtrot. It is still danced stateside under the name of Peabody. The name comes from police lieutenant, William Frank Peabody, from Brooklyn, who helped to popularize the dance.

The dance has progressed and is now more lively. Experienced dancers can make use of Polka rhythms, Charleston, skipping steps and fast syncopation movements. You may have seen on television expert dancers, such as Anton du Beke and Erin Boag, make full use of the scope given to them by the dance. However, do not assume that the dance is only for the skilled. The Quickstep is a simple dance and one that everyone can enjoy, and because it is fairly quick at 48–50 bars a minute, it provides you with excellent exercise. It is more energetic than walking and a few Quicksteps of say three to four minutes each will probably give you as much exercise as walking one mile. Add to that the discipline of learning the steps, and applying what you have learnt, and you have a healthly exercise programme.

HOLD AND TIME This is a dance with a close hold. The music is in 4/4 time (four beats to the bar) and individual steps take up either one or two beats.

Legendary ballroom dancers Irene and Vernon Castle in a typical ballroom hold of the period (*c.*1910).

Chassés Progressing (a preparatory exercise)

This figure is included in order to get you used to the feel of the rhythm and the type of patterns used in this dance. The eight steps, not including the preparatory step, can be repeated.

Man's Steps

Start by facing the nearest wall.

Lady's Steps

Start by backing the nearest wall.

Count:		M		L
Slow	P	LEFT FOOT takes a small step to the side, taking two beats of music.	P	RIGHT FOOT takes a small step to the side, taking two beats of music.
Slow	1	RIGHT FOOT takes a step forwards, taking two beats of music.	1	LEFT FOOT takes a step backwards, taking two beats of music.
Quick	2	LEFT FOOT takes a step to the side along the line parallel with the wall that the right foot is on, taking one beat of music.	2	RIGHT FOOT takes a step to the side along the line parallel with the wall that the left foot is on, taking one beat of music.
Quick	3	RIGHT FOOT closes to left foot, with the weight back onto right foot, taking one beat of music.	3	LEFT FOOT closes to right foot, with the weight back onto the left foot, taking one beat of music.
Slow	4	LEFT FOOT takes a small step to the side, taking two beats of music.	4	RIGHT FOOT takes a small step to the side, taking two beats of music.
Slow	5	RIGHT FOOT takes a step backwards, taking two beats of music.	5	LEFT FOOT takes a step forwards, taking two beats of music.
Quick	6	LEFT FOOT takes a step to the side along the line parallel with wall that the right foot is on, taking one beat of music.	6	RIGHT FOOT takes a step to the side along the line parallel with wall that the left foot is on, taking one beat of music.
Quick	7	RIGHT FOOT closes to left foot, taking one beat of music.	7	LEFT FOOT closes to right foot, taking one beat of music.
Slow	8	LEFT FOOT takes a small step to the side, taking two beats of music.	8	RIGHT FOOT takes a small step to the side, taking two beats of music.

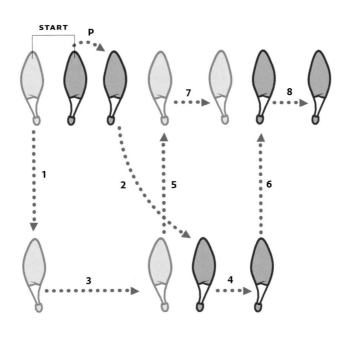

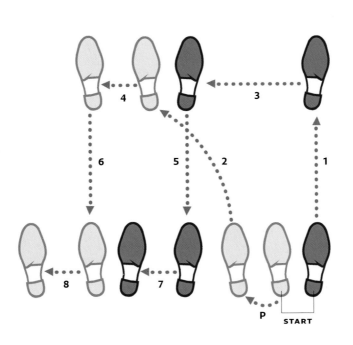

Chassés Progressing (a preparatory exercise)

Slow

P **M** LEFT FOOT takes a small step to the side.
L RIGHT FOOT takes a small step to the side. Takes two beats of music.

Slow

1 **M** RIGHT FOOT takes a step forwards.
L LEFT FOOT takes a step backwards. Takes two beats of music.

Slow

5 **M** RIGHT FOOT takes a step backwards.
L LEFT FOOT takes a step forwards. Takes two beats of music.

Quick

6 **M** LEFT FOOT takes a step to the side.
L RIGHT FOOT takes a step to the side. Takes one beat of music.

Quick

7 **M** RIGHT FOOT closes to left foot.
L LEFT FOOT closes to right foot. Takes one beat of music.

Quick

Quick

Slow

2 **M** LEFT FOOT takes a step
to the side.
L RIGHT FOOT takes a step
to the side.
Takes one beat of music.

3 **M** RIGHT FOOT closes to
left foot.
L LEFT FOOT closes to
right foot.
Takes one beat of music.

4 **M** LEFT FOOT takes a small
step to the side.
L RIGHT FOOT takes a
small step to the side.
Takes two beats of
music.

Slow

8 **M** LEFT FOOT takes a small
step to the side.
L RIGHT FOOT takes a
small step to the side.
Takes two beats of
music.

Quick Feet

The eight steps shown here, not including the preparatory
step, can be repeated.

You might find it helpful to remember the foot patterns
rather than count in Slows and Quicks. The man should
count to himself 'forward, side, close, side, backward, side,
close, side'. The lady should count 'backward, side, close,
side, forward, side, close, side'.

Quarter Turn and Progressive Chassé

Man's Steps

Start by facing the nearest wall and then turn left about 45 degrees – 'facing diagonally to wall'.

Lady's Steps

Start with your back towards the nearest wall and then turn left about 45 degrees – 'backing diagonally to wall'.

Count:		M		L
Slow	P	LEFT FOOT takes a small step to the side.	P	RIGHT FOOT takes a small step to the side.
Slow	1	RIGHT FOOT takes a step forwards, starting to turn right.	1	LEFT FOOT takes a step backwards, starting to turn right.
Quick	2	LEFT FOOT takes a step to the side, turning to the right.	2	RIGHT FOOT takes a step to the side, turning to the right.
Quick	3	RIGHT FOOT closes to left foot, still turning to the right.	3	LEFT FOOT closes to right foot, still turning to the right.
Slow	4	LEFT FOOT takes a small step to the side. You should have turned about a quarter of a turn to the right and be facing slanting out of the room against the direction of the dance ('backing diagonally to centre').	4	RIGHT FOOT takes a small step to the side. You should have turned about a quarter of a turn to the right and be facing slanting into the room and in the direction of the dance ('facing diagonally to centre').
Slow	5	RIGHT FOOT takes a step backwards, starting to turn left.	5	LEFT FOOT takes a step forwards, starting to turn to the left.
Quick	6	LEFT FOOT takes a step to the side, turning to the left.	6	RIGHT FOOT takes a step to the side, turning to the left.
Quick	7	RIGHT FOOT closes to left foot, still turning to the left.	7	LEFT FOOT closes to right foot, still turning to the left.
Slow	8	LEFT FOOT takes a small step to the side. You should have turned about a quarter of a turn to the left and be 'facing diagonally to wall' again.	8	RIGHT FOOT takes a small step to the side. You should have turned about a quarter of a turn to the left and be 'backing diagonally to wall' again.

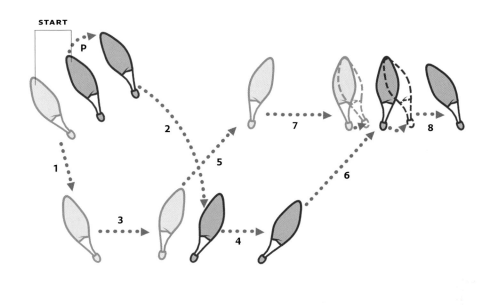

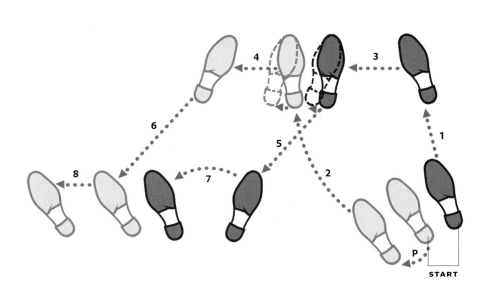

The Forward Lock Step

This is a very popular figure and is ideally followed by any figure commencing on the man's right foot stepping 'outside partner' – this could be the Quarter Turn and Progressive Chassé (see pages 104–5), or Natural Pivot Turn (see pages 112–13), omitting the preparatory steps.

Man's Steps

Start by 'facing diagonally to wall'.

Lady's Steps

Start by 'backing diagonally to wall'.

Count:		M		L
Slow	1	RIGHT FOOT takes a step forwards to your left of both your partner's feet, 'outside partner', onto the heel of your foot.	1	LEFT FOOT takes a small step backwards with your partner stepping to the right of both your feet, 'outside partner'.
Quick	2	LEFT FOOT takes a step forwards, leading with the left side of your body a little and stepping onto the ball of foot, rather than heel.	2	RIGHT FOOT takes a step backwards, leading with the right side of your body a little and not lowering the heel of your foot as the weight is taken onto it.
Quick	3	RIGHT FOOT crosses behind left foot, stepping onto the ball of your right foot so that the weight is carried on the balls of both feet.	3	LEFT FOOT crosses in front of right foot, stepping onto the ball of your left foot so that the weight is carried on the balls of both feet.
Slow	4	LEFT FOOT takes a small step forwards and to the side, still on the balls of your feet, lowering the heel at the end of the step.	4	RIGHT FOOT takes a small step backwards and to the side, still on the balls of your feet, lowering the heel at the end of the step.

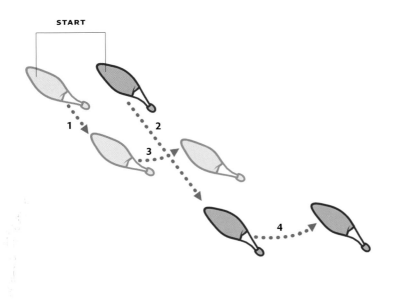

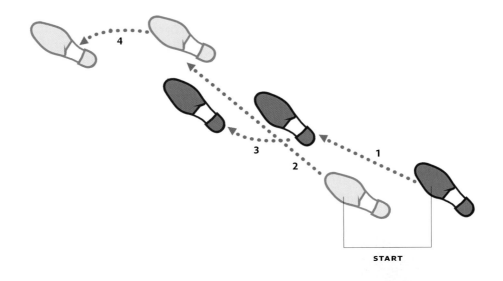

Quarter Turn and Progressive Chassé

Slow *Slow* *Quick*

P **M** LEFT FOOT takes a small step to the side.
L RIGHT FOOT takes a small step to the side.

1 **M** RIGHT FOOT takes a small step forwards, starting to turn right.
L LEFT FOOT takes a small step backwards, starting to turn right.

2 **M** LEFT FOOT takes a step to the side, turning to the right.
L RIGHT FOOT takes a step to the side, turning to the right.

Quick *Slow*

7 **M** RIGHT FOOT closes to left foot, still turning to the left.
L LEFT FOOT closes to right foot, still turning to the left.

8 **M** LEFT FOOT takes a small step to side, completing the turn to the left.
L RIGHT FOOT takes a small step to side, completing the turn to the left.

Repeat Performance

Omitting the preparatory step this figure can be repeated, but step 1 ('right foot forwards' for man and 'left foot backwards' for lady) is taken with the man stepping to his left of the lady's feet. This is called a step 'outside partner'. It can be taken without losing body contact and you should try not to move away from partner as you take the step.

Quick

Slow

Slow

Quick

3 **M** RIGHT FOOT closes to left foot, still turning to the right.
L LEFT FOOT closes to right foot still turning to the right.

4 **M** LEFT FOOT takes a small step to side, completing the turn to the right.
L RIGHT FOOT takes a small step to side, completing the turn to the right.

5 **M** RIGHT FOOT takes a step backwards, starting to turn to the left.
L LEFT FOOT takes a step forwards, starting to turn to the left.

6 **M** LEFT FOOT takes a step to the side, turning to the left.
L RIGHT FOOT takes a step to the side, turning to the left.

The Forward Lock Step

Slow

Quick

Quick

Slow

1 **M** RIGHT FOOT a small step forwards, 'outside partner', onto heel.
L LEFT FOOT a small step backwards, 'partner outside', lowering heel.

2 **M** LEFT FOOT forwards, leading with left side and stepping onto ball of foot.
L RIGHT FOOT backwards, leading with right side, and heel is not lowered.

3 **M** RIGHT FOOT crosses behind left foot, weight is on balls of feet.
L LEFT FOOT crosses in front of right foot, weight is on balls of feet.

4 **M** LEFT FOOT forwards and to the side.
L RIGHT FOOT backwards and to the side. Both man and lady still on balls of feet, lowering heels at the end of step.

A series of photographic stills taken from the 1935 film, *Top Hat*, starring Fred Astaire and Ginger Rogers.

The Natural Pivot Turn

This figure is useful when you are approaching a corner, because when you have completed it, you are in a position to move along the next side of the room. It is a little more difficult, but is a very valuable dancing asset and worth a little extra effort. Follow this figure with the Quarter Turn and Progressive Chassé (see pages 104–5), omitting the preparatory step.

Man's Steps

Start by 'facing diagonally to wall A', that is, stand with your right side or shoulder pointing towards the nearest wall and turn 45 degrees to your right.

Lady's Steps

Start by 'backing diagonally to wall A', that is, stand with your left side or shoulder pointing towards the nearest wall and turn 45 degrees to your right.

Count:		M		L
Slow	P	LEFT FOOT takes a small step to the side.	P	RIGHT FOOT takes a small step to the side.
Slow	1	RIGHT FOOT takes a step forwards, turning to the right.	1	LEFT FOOT takes a step backwards, turning to the right.
Quick	2	LEFT FOOT takes a step to the side, still turning to the right.	2	RIGHT FOOT takes a step to the side, still turning to right.
Quick	3	RIGHT FOOT closes to left foot, still turning to the right. By now your left side should be pointing towards wall A and your back should be backing wall B.	3	LEFT FOOT closes to right foot, still turning to the right. By now your right side should be pointing towards wall A and you should be facing wall B.
Slow	4	LEFT FOOT takes a step backwards and leftwards, turning strongly to the right on the ball of your foot, but with your heel close to the floor and leaving your right foot forwards in front of your left foot. Turn sufficiently so that you are now 'facing diagonally to wall B'.	4	RIGHT FOOT takes a step forwards, turning strongly to the right on the ball of your foot, but with your heel close to the floor and leaving your left foot backwards behind your right foot. Turn sufficiently so that you are now 'backing diagonally to wall B'.

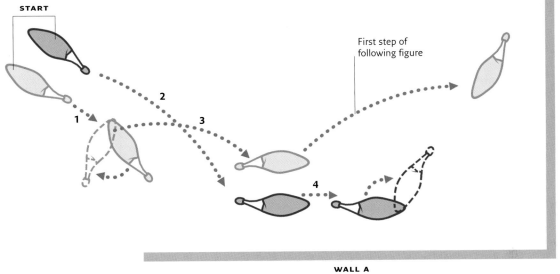

START

1

2

3

4

First step of following figure

WALL A

WALL B

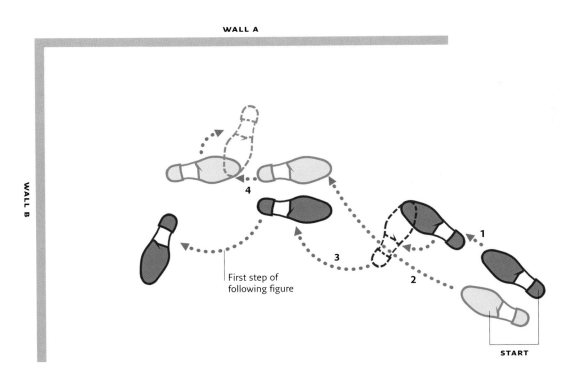

WALL A

WALL B

4

3

2

1

START

First step of following figure

Quick Open Reverse Turn with Progressive Chassé Ending

When it is not danced at a corner, you can precede this figure with a Quarter Turn and Progressive Chassé (see pages 104–5) turned strongly to the left to finish 'facing diagonally to centre', followed by one forwards step on the man's right foot, 'outside partner', or with the Natural Pivot Turn (see pages 112–13) and one forwards step on the man's right foot. Follow with either a Quarter Turn and Progressive Chassé, a Natural Pivot Turn or a Forward Lock Step (see pages 106–7), commencing with the man's right foot taking a small step forwards to his left of the lady's feet, that is, 'outside partner'.

Man's Steps

Start by 'facing diagonally to centre'.

Lady's Steps

Start by 'backing diagonally to centre'.

Count:		M		L
Slow	1	LEFT FOOT takes a step forwards, turning to the left.	1	RIGHT FOOT takes a step backwards, turning to the left.
Quick	2	RIGHT FOOT takes a small step to the side, still turning to the left.	2	LEFT FOOT takes a step to the side, still turning to the left.
Quick	3	LEFT FOOT takes a step backwards, still turning left and leading the lady to step to the right of both your feet, 'partner outside'. You should now be facing down the room against the direction of the dance, with your left shoulder pointing towards the nearest wall.	3	RIGHT FOOT takes a step forwards, still turning left and stepping to your left of both your partner's feet, 'outside partner'. You should now be facing down the room in the direction of the dance with your right shoulder pointing towards the nearest wall.
Slow	4	RIGHT FOOT takes a step backwards, still turning to the left.	4	LEFT FOOT takes a step forwards, still turning to the left.
Quick	5	LEFT FOOT takes a step to the side, still turning to the left, now facing the nearest wall.	5	RIGHT FOOT takes a step to the side, still turning left, now with back towards the nearest wall.
Quick	6	RIGHT FOOT closes to left foot, completing the turn to the left.	6	LEFT FOOT closes to right foot, completing the turn to the left.
Slow	7	LEFT FOOT takes a small step to the side, preparing to step 'outside partner' on the next step.	7	RIGHT FOOT takes a small step to the side.

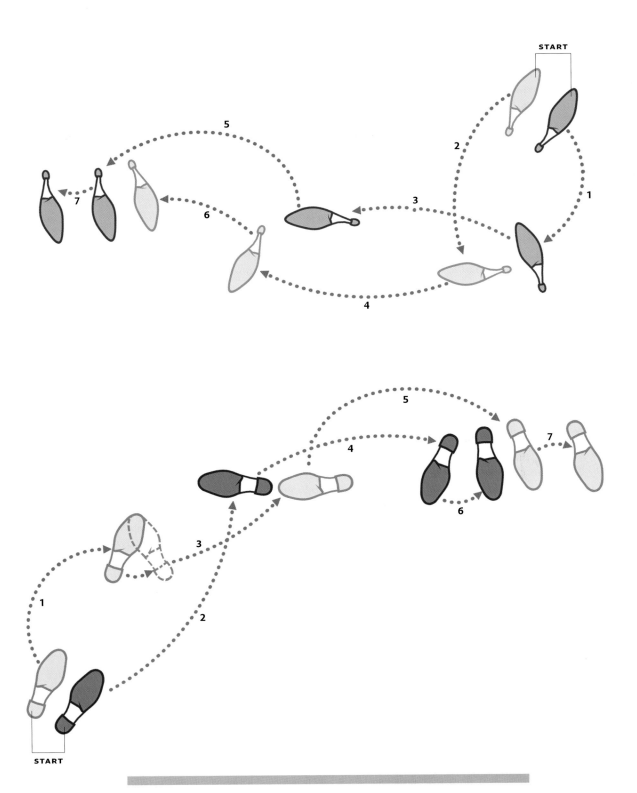

The Natural Pivot Turn

Slow

Slow

Quick

P **M** LEFT FOOT takes a small step to the side.
L RIGHT FOOT takes a small step to the side.

1 **M** RIGHT FOOT takes a step forwards, turning to the right.
L LEFT FOOT takes a step backwards, turning to the right.

2 **M** LEFT FOOT takes a step to side, still turning to the right.
L RIGHT FOOT takes a step to side, still turning to the right.

Quick Open Reverse Turn with Progressive Chassé Ending

Slow

Quick

Quick

1 **M** LEFT FOOT takes a step forwards, turning to the left.
L RIGHT FOOT takes a step backwards, turning to the left.

2 **M** RIGHT FOOT takes a step to the side, still turning to left.
L LEFT FOOT takes a step to the side, still turning to left.

3 **M** LEFT FOOT backwards, still turning to the left, leading lady to step 'outside partner'.
L RIGHT FOOT forwards, still turning to the left.

Quick

Slow

Finish

3 **M** RIGHT FOOT closes to left foot, still turning to the right.
L LEFT FOOT closes to right foot still turning to the right.

4 **M** LEFT FOOT takes a step backwards and to the left, turning strongly to the right.
L RIGHT FOOT takes a step forwards, turning strongly to the right.

F Position reached after the strong turn to the right. Both man and lady finish facing a little to the right of a line running parallel to the new wall.

Slow

Quick

Quick

Slow

4 **M** RIGHT FOOT takes a step backwards, still turning to the left.
L LEFT FOOT takes a step forwards, still turning to the left.

5 **M** LEFT FOOT a step to side, still turning left, now facing nearest wall.
L RIGHT FOOT a step to side, still turning left, now with back towards nearest wall.

6 **M** RIGHT FOOT closes to left foot, completing turn to left.
L LEFT FOOT closes to right foot, completing turn to left.

7 **M** LEFT FOOT takes a small step to the side, preparing to step 'outside partner' on the next step.
L RIGHT FOOT takes a small step to the side.

Rock 'n' Roll and Jive

Jill Halfpenny and Darren Bennet jive dancing to secure their place as winners of the second series of BBC TV's *Strictly Come Dancing* competition.

The majority of popular dances, if not all, develop from the dancing public and are not generally an invention of any one person. It is a strange process and difficult to track down. For instance, in the early 1940s, British youth took to Jitterbugging, which in itself is a precursor of Rock 'n' Roll and Jive.

Rock 'n' Roll music has its roots in rhythm-and-blues, which was first played by black musicians in the USA in the late 1920s onwards. Later, in the mid-1930s, the Boswell Sisters had success with the song 'Rock and Roll' – predating the phenomenon of Rock 'n' Roll by nearly 20 years. Similarly, 'Rock it for Me' was recorded by several bands in 1937 and dancers began to exploit the positive rhythms. The impact of these trends was felt when American Forces were based in Britain during World War II. Their presence transformed the ballrooms, which began to promote energetic big bands, encouraging

Elvis Presley, the King of Rock, shakes his infamous hips in the film *Jailhouse Rock* in 1957.

A prison show gives Elvis Presley his first opportunity to sing and dance

M-G-M Presents "**JAILHOUSE ROCK**" CinemaScope

Olivia Newton-John and John Travolta jiving at Rydell High's prom, in the 1978 popular dance film, *Grease*.

wild dancing and virtuoso improvisation. For the safety of other dancers it was necessary to place some restrictions on what dancers could perform. Some dancehalls even carried notices stating 'No Jitterbugging'.

JIVE TO ROCK Rock 'n' Roll was gradually becoming acceptable and dance teachers codified the dance, using the name Jive. With the success of a new breed of dance band – the rock group – Rock 'n' Roll was firmly established. Prior to the post-War years, bands had been fairly large, commonly up to 14 musicians who played melodious tunes. The rock bands were smaller, concentrated more on rhythm instruments and with less emphasis on tune.

The major impact was that of Bill Haley and the Comets with his recording of 'Rock Around The Clock' in 1954. When he appeared in theatres, the aisles were full of youngsters dancing. Elvis Presley cemented the original impact with tunes such as 'All Shook Up'. Many popular modern music tunes, with their emphasis on heavy, insistent rhythms are excellent for Rock 'n' Roll and Jive, as well as other variants now to be seen.

ROCK 'N' ROLL RHYTHMS When the dance was first analysed, three optional rhythms were identified that can be characterized as single, double and triple step types. Jive uses the triple rhythm unit while Rock 'n' Roll uses the single. As you might expect, the different rhythms (units) create a distinctive character for each dance. However, nearly all figures in one style can be danced in the other and vice versa.

Firstly, some figures in Rock 'n' Roll format are described and, secondly, it is shown how they can be danced in Jive. The Rock 'n' Roll format has been chosen as the starting form because it is believed to be slightly easier, and is most favoured by social dancers. There may be places where the instructions given contradict the technique accepted by most dance authorities. Instructions have been written in such a way as to make the figures easy for the beginner.

THE HOLD This is a relaxed dance with a casual Open Hold (see page 18). Because there is no body contact it is important to remember that the guide from the man has to come through his hands.

Rock 'n' Roll Rhythm Basic

There is very little movement across the floor over these steps and each group of three steps is rather like a shuffle. The important aspect is to try and feel the accents in the music on the second and fourth beats of the bar and express them with extra pressure into the floor whenever possible. The Quick steps in Rock 'n' Roll take one beat of music and the Slow steps take two beats. Commence in Open Hold.

Man's Steps

Lady's Steps

Count:		**M**		**L**
Quick	1	LEFT FOOT takes a step to the left, taking one beat of music.	1	RIGHT FOOT takes a step to the right, taking one beat of music.
Quick	2	RIGHT FOOT closes towards the left foot, taking one beat of music.	2	LEFT FOOT closes towards the right foot, taking one beat of music.
Slow	3	LEFT FOOT takes a tiny step to the left, increasing the pressure on the foot during the second half of the step, taking two beats of music.	3	RIGHT FOOT takes a tiny step to the right, increasing the pressure on the foot during second half of the step, taking two beats of music.
Quick	4	RIGHT FOOT takes a tiny step to the right, taking one beat of music.	4	LEFT FOOT takes a tiny step to the left, taking one beat of music.
Quick	5	LEFT FOOT closes towards the right foot, taking one beat of music.	5	RIGHT FOOT closes towards the left foot, taking one beat of music.
Slow	6	RIGHT FOOT takes a tiny step to the right, increasing the pressure on the foot during the second half of the step, taking two beats of music.	6	LEFT FOOT takes a tiny step to the left, increasing the pressure on the foot during the second half of the step, taking two beats of music.

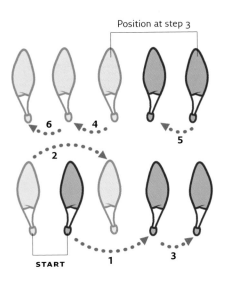

Position at step 3

6 4

2

5

1 3

START

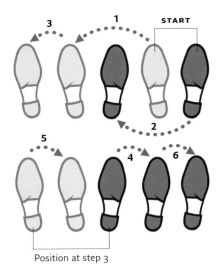

3 1 START

2

5 4 6

Position at step 3

Fall-away Rhythm Basic

Once you have danced the first six steps of the Rhythm Basic (see pages 122–3) you can follow it with Fall-away Rhythm Basic. These four steps can be repeated as often as you fancy. Commence in Open Hold.

		Man's Steps		Lady's Steps
Count:		**M**		**L**
Quick	1	LEFT FOOT takes a step backwards, turning to the left so that your left side moves away from the lady's right side, making a V shape.	1	RIGHT FOOT takes a step backwards, turning to the right so that your right side moves away from the man's left side, making a V shape.
Quick	2	RIGHT FOOT remains in place and weight is taken firmly forwards onto it, starting to turn right to face your partner again.	2	LEFT FOOT remains in place and weight is taken firmly forwards onto it, beginning to turn left to face towards partner again.
Slow	3	LEFT FOOT takes a small step to the side, turning right to face your partner, increasing pressure on foot during the second half of the step.	3	RIGHT FOOT takes a small step to the side, turning left to face your partner, increasing pressure on foot during the second half of the step.
Slow	4	RIGHT FOOT takes a tiny step towards the left foot, increasing pressure on the foot at the end of the step.	4	LEFT FOOT takes a tiny step towards the right foot, increasing pressure on the foot during the second half of the step.

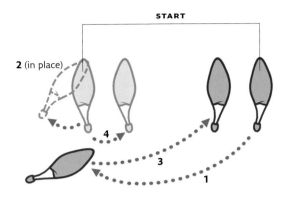

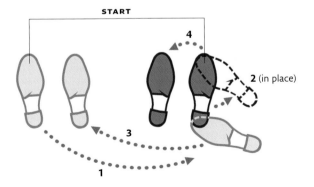

Rock 'n' Roll Rhythm Basic

Quick

Quick

Slow

1 **M** LEFT FOOT takes a step to the left.
L RIGHT FOOT takes a step to the right.

2 **M** RIGHT FOOT closes towards the left foot.
L LEFT FOOT closes towards the right foot.

3 **M** LEFT FOOT takes a tiny step to left, increasing pressure on foot.
L RIGHT FOOT takes a tiny step to right, increasing pressure on foot.

Fall-away Rhythm Basic

Quick

Quick

1 **M** LEFT FOOT backwards, turning to the left.
L RIGHT FOOT backwards turning to the right so that your right side moves away from the man's left side.

2 **M** RIGHT FOOT remains in place, taking weight onto it, starting to turn right.
L LEFT FOOT remains in place, taking weight onto it, starting to turn left to face towards partner.

Quick

Quick

Slow

4 **M** RIGHT FOOT takes a tiny
step to the right.
L LEFT FOOT takes a tiny
step to the left.

5 **M** LEFT FOOT closes
towards the right foot.
L RIGHT FOOT closes
towards the left foot.

6 **M** RIGHT FOOT takes a tiny
step to right, increasing
pressure on foot.
L LEFT FOOT takes a tiny
step to left, increasing
pressure on foot.

Slow

Slow

3 **M** LEFT FOOT a small step
to side, turning to right,
with pressure on foot.
L RIGHT FOOT a small step
to side, turning to left to
face partner, with
pressure on foot.

4 **M** RIGHT FOOT takes a tiny
step towards left foot,
with pressure on foot.
L LEFT FOOT takes a tiny
step towards right foot,
with pressure on foot.

Promenade Walks

This figure can be danced after steps 1–6 of the Rock 'n' Roll Rhythm Basic or the Fall-away Rhythm Basic (see pages 122–7). It can be followed by steps 4–6 of the Rhythm Basic.

	Count:	**Man's Steps** — M		**Lady's Steps** — L
Quick	1	LEFT FOOT takes a step backwards, turning to the left so that you move further away from the lady's right side, making a V shape.	1	RIGHT FOOT takes a step backwards, turning to the right so that you move further away from the man's left side, making a V shape.
Quick	2	RIGHT FOOT remains in place and the weight is taken firmly forwards onto it.	2	LEFT FOOT remains in place and weight is taken firmly forwards onto it.
Slow	3	LEFT FOOT takes a step to the side in promenade position, increasing the pressure on the foot at the end of the step.	3	RIGHT FOOT takes a step to the side in promenade position, increasing the pressure on the foot at the end of the step.
Quick	4	RIGHT FOOT takes a step forwards and across left foot, still in promenade position.	4	LEFT FOOT takes a step forwards and across right foot, still in promenade position.
Quick	5	LEFT FOOT takes a step to the side of right foot, still in promenade position.	5	RIGHT FOOT takes a step to the side of left foot, still in promenade position.
Slow	6	RIGHT FOOT takes a small step forwards and across left foot, still in promenade position and increasing pressure on the foot.	6	LEFT FOOT takes a small step forwards and across right foot, still in promenade position and increasing pressure on the foot.
Quick	7	LEFT FOOT takes a step to the side, turning a little to the right but not so much as to face partner.	7	RIGHT FOOT takes a step to the side, turning a little to the left but not so much as to face partner.
Quick	8	RIGHT FOOT takes a small step towards left foot.	8	LEFT FOOT takes a small step towards the right foot.
Slow	9	LEFT FOOT takes a step to the side, now facing partner and increasing pressure on the foot at end of the step.	9	RIGHT FOOT takes a step to the side, now facing partner and increasing pressure on the foot at the end of the step.

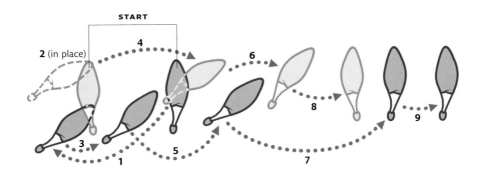

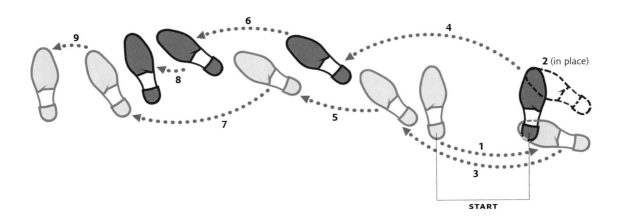

Promenade Walks

Quick

Quick

Slow

1 **M** LEFT FOOT backwards turning to left, moving away from lady's right side.
L RIGHT FOOT backwards turning to right, moving away from man's left side.

2 **M** RIGHT FOOT remains in place and weight is taken firmly onto it.
L LEFT FOOT remains in place and weight is taken firmly onto it.

3 **M** LEFT FOOT takes a step to the side in promenade position.
L RIGHT FOOT takes a step to the side in promenade position.

Quick

Quick

Slow

7 **M** LEFT FOOT takes a step to side, turning slightly to the right.
L RIGHT FOOT takes a step to side, turning slightly to the left.

8 **M** RIGHT FOOT takes a small step towards the left foot.
L LEFT FOOT takes a small step towards the right foot.

9 **M** LEFT FOOT takes a step to the side, now facing partner.
L RIGHT FOOT takes a step to the side, now facing partner.

Quick

Quick

Slow

4 **M** RIGHT FOOT takes a step forwards and across left foot.
L LEFT FOOT takes a step forwards and across right foot. Both still in promenade position.

5 **M** LEFT FOOT takes a step to side of right foot.
L RIGHT FOOT takes a step to side of left. Both still in promenade position.

6 **M** RIGHT FOOT takes a small step forwards and across left foot.
L LEFT FOOT takes a small step forwards and across right foot. Still in promenade position.

Modern, popular music with its emphasis on heavy, insistent rhythms is excellent for Rock 'n' Roll and Jive dancing as well as other variants now to be seen.

A couple throw themselves into an acrobatic jive in the 1950s, illustrating the sort of movement that caused dance hall owners to try and ban the dance due to possible harm to other dancers.

Underarm Turn to Right for Lady

Dance this figure after the Promenade Walks (see pages 128–31) and steps 4–6 of the Rhythm Basic (see pages 122–3). You can follow it with the Link (see pages 136–7).

	Count:	**Man's Steps** M		**Lady's Steps** L
Quick	1	LEFT FOOT takes a step backwards, turning to the left so that your left side moves further away from the lady's right side, making a small V shape.	1	RIGHT FOOT takes a step backwards, turning to the right so that your right side moves further away from the man's left side, making a small V shape.
Quick	2	RIGHT FOOT remains in place, weight is taken firmly forwards onto it. Start turning the lady a little to her left by pressure with the right hand and begin to raise your left hand.	2	LEFT FOOT remains in place, weight is taken firmly forwards onto it and start turning a little to your left.
Slow	3	LEFT FOOT takes a small step to the side, then turning to your left after a brief pause, turn the lady to her right under your left and her right hand. Do not grip the lady's hand too tightly but allow her to turn.	3	RIGHT FOOT takes a step to the side, turning to the left but with your right side still away from your partner. Press into the floor and spin on the ball of your right foot about three quarters of a full turn to the right to face your partner.
Slow	4	RIGHT FOOT takes a small step to the side, completing the turn to your left.	4	LEFT FOOT takes a small step backwards, completing the turn to your right.

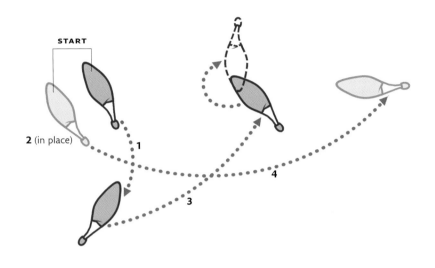

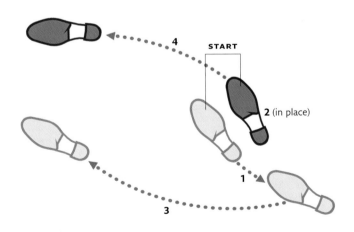

The Link

This figure is used to bring partners together in normal hold with the man holding the lady's right hand in his left hand, after they have been separated. The man stands with the weight on his right foot and the lady with the weight on her left foot. Dance the Link after the Underarm Turn to Right for Lady (see pages 134–5).

		Man's Steps		**Lady's Steps**

Count:		**M**		**L**
Quick	1	LEFT FOOT takes a small step backwards.	1	RIGHT FOOT takes a small step backwards.
Quick	2	RIGHT FOOT remains in place and weight is taken firmly forwards onto it.	2	LEFT FOOT remains in place and weight is taken firmly forwards onto it.
Slow	3	LEFT FOOT takes a small step forwards, drawing partner towards you to regain normal hold.	3	RIGHT FOOT takes a small step forwards towards partner, to regain normal hold.
Slow	4	RIGHT FOOT takes a small step to the side in normal hold.	4	LEFT FOOT takes a small step to the side in normal hold.

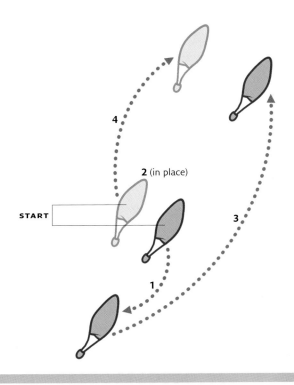

2 (in place)

START

4

3

1

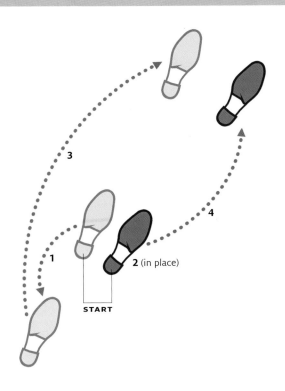

3

1

4

2 (in place)

START

The Link in Jive Rhythm

All of the figures in the Rock 'n' Roll section can be danced with Jive Rhythm. Whenever there is a step that is counted 'slow', replace that step with three by counting 'Quick a Quick'. The precise beat value for that phrase is ¾, ¼,1, making two beats or half a bar of common time music. The phrase 'quick a quick' does not fully convey the right feeling and if you think to yourself 'da de dah', with emphasis on the 'dah', that might help. The inclusion of this triplet in Jive gives the dance a lighter, bubbly character and one can truly be said to be 'tripping the light fantastic'. By contrast in Rock 'n' Roll, as a result of the pressure into the floor in the second half of the slow steps, the character is more solid or gutsy.

The Link is described in Rock 'n' Roll style on pages 136–7, here the instructions are given for dancing this figure to a Jive rhythm. This should enable you to make the same transposition for all the Rock 'n' Roll figures if you want to do so.

	Count:	**M** — Man's Steps		**L** — Lady's Steps
Quick	1	LEFT FOOT takes a small step backwards.	1	RIGHT FOOT takes a small step backwards.
Quick	2	RIGHT FOOT remains in place and the weight is taken onto it.	2	LEFT FOOT remains in place and the weight is taken onto it.
Quick	3	LEFT FOOT takes a small step forwards, starting to draw your partner towards you.	3	RIGHT FOOT takes a small step forwards, towards your partner.
a	4	RIGHT FOOT closes towards left foot, still drawing partner towards you.	4	LEFT FOOT closes towards right foot.
Quick	5	LEFT FOOT takes a small step forwards, regaining normal hold.	5	RIGHT FOOT takes a small step forwards, regaining normal hold.
Quick	6	RIGHT FOOT takes a small step to the side.	6	LEFT FOOT takes a small step to the side.
a	7	LEFT FOOT closes towards right foot.	7	RIGHT FOOT closes towards left foot.
Quick	8	RIGHT FOOT takes a small step to the side.	8	LEFT FOOT takes a small step to the side.

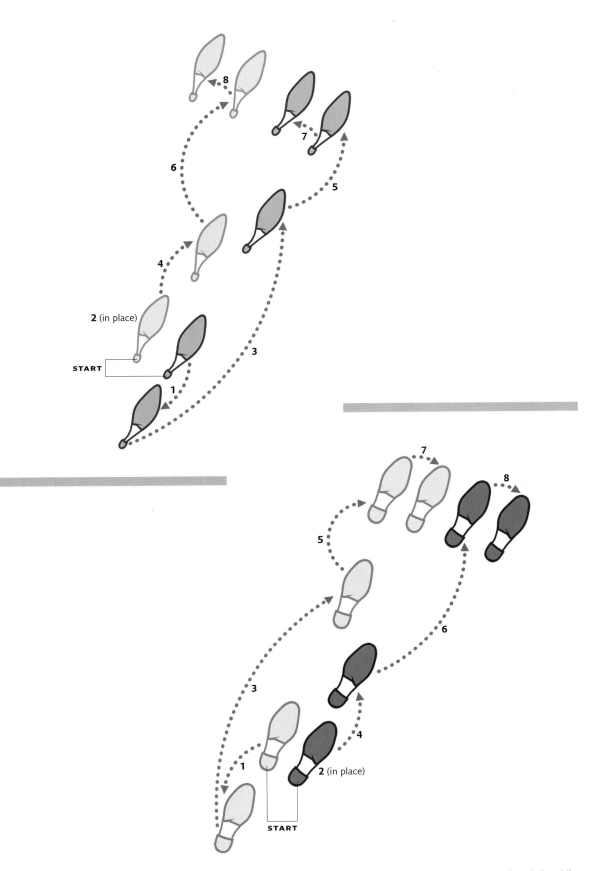

2 (in place)

START

1

3

4

5

6

7

8

7

8

5

3

6

1

4

2 (in place)

START

Underarm Turn to Right for Lady

Quick

Quick

Slow

Slow

1 **M** LEFT FOOT backwards, turning to left, moving away from lady's right side.
L RIGHT FOOT backwards. turning to right, moving away from man's left side.

2 **M** RIGHT FOOT remains in place, weight taken onto it, turning lady to left. Start to raise left hand.
L LEFT FOOT remains in place, weight taken onto it, start turning to left.

3 **M** LEFT FOOT a step to side, turning lady to her right.
L RIGHT FOOT a step to the side turning left, then spin on the ball of your foot to the right until you face your partner.

4 **M** RIGHT FOOT takes a small step to the side, turning to your left.
L LEFT FOOT takes a small step backwards, completing the turn to your right.

The Link in Jive Rhythm

Quick

Quick

Quick

a

1 **M** LEFT FOOT takes a small step backwards.
L RIGHT FOOT takes a small step backwards.

2 **M** RIGHT FOOT remains in place and weight is taken onto it.
L LEFT FOOT remains in place and weight is taken onto it.

3 **M** LEFT FOOT takes a small step forwards, starting to draw your partner towards you.
L RIGHT FOOT takes a small step forwards.

4 **M** RIGHT FOOT closes towards left foot, still drawing your partner towards you.
L LEFT FOOT closes towards right foot.

The Link

Quick

Quick

Slow

Slow

1 **M** LEFT FOOT takes a small step backwards.
L RIGHT FOOT takes a small step backwards.

2 **M** RIGHT FOOT remains in place and weight is taken firmly forwards onto it.
L LEFT FOOT remains in place and weight is taken firmly forwards onto it.

3 **M** LEFT FOOT takes a small step forwards, drawing the lady towards you to regain normal hold.
L RIGHT FOOT takes a small step forwards, to regain normal hold.

4 **M** RIGHT FOOT takes a small step to the side in normal hold.
L LEFT FOOT takes a small step to the side in normal hold.

Quick

Quick

a

Quick

5 **M** LEFT FOOT takes a small step forwards, regaining normal hold.
L RIGHT FOOT takes a small step forwards, regaining normal hold.

6 **M** RIGHT FOOT takes a small step to the side.
L LEFT FOOT takes a small step to the side.

7 **M** LEFT FOOT closes towards right foot.
L RIGHT FOOT closes towards left foot.

8 **M** RIGHT FOOT takes a small step to the side.
L LEFT FOOT takes a small step to the side.

Jive Changes of Place, Right to Left

This figure precedes Jive Changes of Place, Left to Right (see pages 144–7). In the amalgamation of these two figures, the lady turns under the arch formed by the man's left and the lady's right joined hands. Each person moves away a little from their partner and then reverses the movement.

	Count:	**Man's Steps**		**Lady's Steps**
		M		**L**
Quick	1	LEFT FOOT backwards, turning to the left so that your left side moves further away from the lady's right side, making a small V shape.	1	RIGHT FOOT backwards, turning to the right so that your right side moves further away from the man's left side, making a small V shape.
Quick	2	RIGHT FOOT remains in place and weight is taken onto it, start turning the lady a little to her left with pressure from your right hand.	2	LEFT FOOT remains in place and weight is taken onto it, start turning a little to the left.
Quick	3	LEFT FOOT takes a small step to the side, turning to your right and turning the lady to her left. She should now be nearly facing you.	3	RIGHT FOOT takes a step to the side, turning left but with your right side still away from partner a little.
a	4	RIGHT FOOT closes a little way towards left foot, starting to raise your left and lady's right hand.	4	LEFT FOOT takes a small step towards the right foot.
Quick	5	LEFT FOOT takes a small step to the side, left hand raised, turning the lady to her right and guiding her by using a clockwise rotation of your left hand, which holds the lady's right hand loosely above her head.	5	RIGHT FOOT takes a small step to the side, starting a strong turn to the right.
Quick	6	RIGHT FOOT takes a small step to the side, turning to your left and finish the lady's strong turn to her right.	6	LEFT FOOT takes a small step to the side and backwards, completing the strong turn to the right.
a	7	LEFT FOOT closes a little way towards the right foot.	7	RIGHT FOOT takes a small step towards the left foot, still turning to the right.
Quick	8	RIGHT FOOT forwards, by now the lady will be facing you, drop the lady's right hand to waist level, still leaving your right hand free.	8	LEFT FOOT takes a small step to the side and backwards, you are now facing your partner.

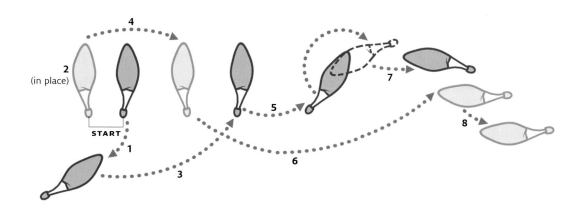

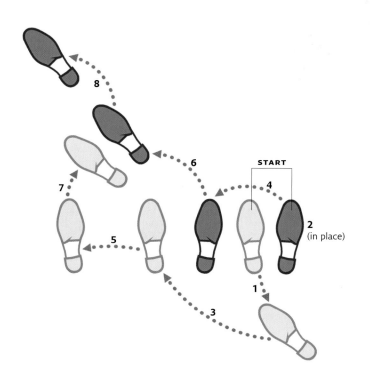

Jive Changes of Place, Left to Right

Follow the Jive Changes of Place, Right to Left (see pages 142–3) with the Changes of Place, Left to Right.

		Man's Steps	**Lady's Steps**

Man's Steps

Lady's Steps

Count:		**M**		**L**
Quick	1	LEFT FOOT takes a small step backwards.	1	RIGHT FOOT takes a small step backwards.
Quick	2	RIGHT FOOT remains in place and weight is taken onto it, starting to turn a little to the right and to raise your left arm.	2	LEFT FOOT remains in place and weight is taken onto it, starting to turn to the left.
Quick	3	LEFT FOOT takes a step to the side, turning a little more to the right and continuing to raise your left arm so as to turn the lady to her left using an anti-clockwise rotation of your left hand.	3	RIGHT FOOT takes a step to the side, turning to the left under the joined hands above your head.
a	4	RIGHT FOOT takes a small step towards left foot, still turning to the right and turning the lady to her left.	4	LEFT FOOT closes a little way towards right foot, still turning to the left.
Quick	5	LEFT FOOT takes a step to the side, still turning to the right and turning the lady to her left.	5	RIGHT FOOT takes a small step to the side, still turning to the left.
Quick	6	RIGHT FOOT takes a small step forwards, the lady now faces you.	6	LEFT FOOT takes a step backwards, you are now facing the man.
a	7	LEFT FOOT takes a small step towards right foot.	7	RIGHT FOOT closes towards left foot.
Quick	8	RIGHT FOOT takes a small step forwards.	8	LEFT FOOT takes a small step backwards.

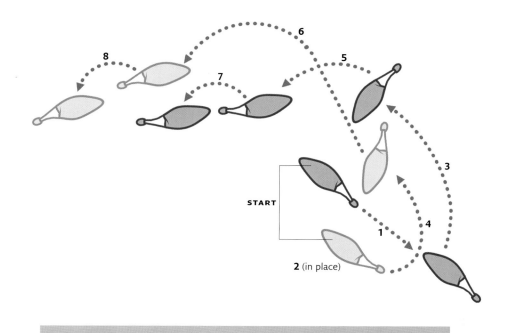

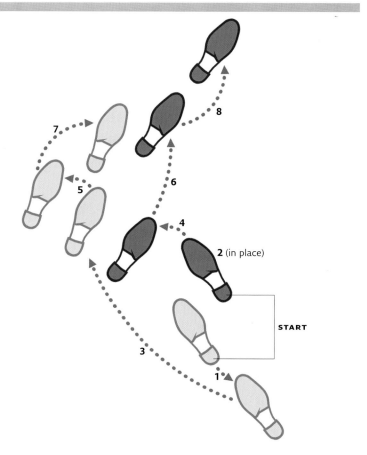

Jive Changes of Place, Right to Left

Quick   *Quick*   *Quick*   *a*

1 **M** LEFT FOOT takes a step backwards, turning to left, moving away from lady's right side.
L RIGHT FOOT backwards, turning to right, moving away from man's left side.

2 **M** RIGHT FOOT remains in place, weight taken onto it, turning lady to her left.
L LEFT FOOT remains in place, weight taken onto it, turning a little to left.

3 **M** LEFT FOOT takes a small step to side, turning to your right and turning lady to her left.
L RIGHT FOOT takes a step to side, turning left but still away from partner.

4 **M** RIGHT FOOT closes a little way towards left foot, starting to raise left and lady's right hand.
L LEFT FOOT a small step towards right foot.

Jive Changes of Place, Left to Right

Quick   *Quick*   *Quick*   *a*

1 **M** LEFT FOOT takes a small step backwards.
L RIGHT FOOT takes a small step backwards.

2 **M** RIGHT FOOT remains in place, weight taken onto it, starting to turn right.
L LEFT FOOT remains in place, weight is taken onto it, start turning left.

3 **M** LEFT FOOT to the side, turning a little more to right and continuing to turn lady to her left.
L RIGHT FOOT to the side, turning to the left under joined hands.

4 **M** RIGHT FOOT takes a small step towards left foot, still turning lady to her left.
L LEFT FOOT closes a little way towards right foot, still turning left.

5 **M** LEFT FOOT takes a small step to side, turning lady to her right with left hand.
L RIGHT FOOT takes a small step to the side, starting a strong turn to the right.

6 **M** RIGHT FOOT a small step to the side, completing the lady's turn to right.
L LEFT FOOT takes a small step to the side and backwards, completing strong turn to the right.

7 **M** LEFT FOOT closes a little way towards right foot.
L RIGHT FOOT a small step towards left foot, still turning right.

8 **M** RIGHT FOOT forwards, lady now facing you, still holding her right hand that can now drop to waist level.
L LEFT FOOT to side and back, now facing partner.

Quick   *Quick*   *a*   *Quick*

5 **M** LEFT FOOT takes a step to the side, still turning lady to her left.
L RIGHT FOOT takes a small step to the side, still turning left.

6 **M** RIGHT FOOT takes a small step forwards, the lady now faces you.
L LEFT FOOT takes a step backwards, you are now facing the man.

7 **M** LEFT FOOT takes a small step towards right foot.
L RIGHT FOOT closes towards left foot.

8 **M** RIGHT FOOT takes a small step forwards.
L LEFT FOOT takes a small step backwards.

Samba

The School of Samba procession in the Rio de Janeiro Carnival in Brazil.

You could say that it all started over 500 years ago, in 1500, when the Spaniard, Vincente Yániez Pinzon, became the first European to land in Brazil. Four months later the country was claimed for Portugal by Pedro Alvarez Cabral, establishing the first settlement at Salvador de Bahia.

What on earth has this to do with a popular dance form, you could well ask? The reason is that national dances are often a microcosm of a country's history, and this is never so apparent than with Brazil and its national dance, the Samba. As is so often the case, the term is really a generic one for a wide range of dances that are all closely related and share the same historical background.

Following the appropriation of the country, many Portuguese people moved to Brazil and brought with them the historical music and dance forms of their native country. As a consequence of the annexation of South American countries came the deplorable importation of slaves from Africa. This resulted in the country becoming a mix of three cultures. The native Brazilian Indians had long established religions, many of a voodoo nature, such as Macumba and its religious dance ceremonies and music. However, the native Indians were treated very badly by the invaders, and little of their culture had a major impact upon the development of today's dance forms.

As mentioned, to the melting pot of dance came the traditional dance and music culture of Portugal. Of particular interest are Fados and Folias. Fado means fate, and the guitar-based music has a wistful character. Folias are expressive dance forms. One striking aspect is that they feature large, extravagant head-dresses – they can hardly be called hats – for the women. Perhaps this could be the historical foundation for the highly elaborate creations worn by the women in the Rio carnival parade each year.

OUT OF AFRICA The major impact on the music and dance comes from the influx of slaves who brought with them their traditional music and dance forms. Slavery was not abolished in Brazil until 1888 and for the greater part of almost 400 years something like 10,000 slaves a year were imported from Africa. They came from Angola, Congo, Dahoney, Guinea, Mozambique, Nigeria, and West Sudan. However, they were mainly of the Mbundu and Ovinbundu tribes of Angola. With them they brought their often sophisticated tribal dances and rhythm instruments. The rhythm instruments were largely crude but very effective, comprising various drums, pandeiros (tambourines), chocallos (hollow tubes filled with hard seeds and shaken to give a very special noise), livros (cigar boxes struck with a stick like a drum) and many more, all of them inexpensive and very easy to make.

They also brought many tribal dances with them, including the Batuque and the Semba. With time these have blended with the Portuguese and native Indian dances to form the dance we now call Samba.

CARNIVAL TIME At the heart of Brazilian culture is the exhilarating spectacle of the Mardi Gras carnival in Rio de Janeiro. This happens on each Shrove Tuesday, which is followed the day after by fasting for Lent. Carnival means 'farewell to meat', and is marked with revelry to fortify oneself for the 40 bleak days to come. Nowhere in the world are the festivities marking the event celebrated as much as they are in Brazil. On Shrove Tuesday a magnificent parade passes through Rio de Janeiro – everyone dances joyfully and wears fantastic costumes and especially

Dancer in a festive costume in the Sambadrome at the Rio de Janeiro Carnival, Brazil.

huge and flamboyant head-dresses. If you have seen Carmen Miranda in one of her films, you will have an idea of the type of head gear referred to.

One of the most spectacular aspects of the Rio procession is the part that contains groups of dancers, the so-called 'escolas de samba' or 'samba schools'. Immediately after Mardi Gras the schools start working on a theme and dances for the next year's procession. At the end of the year they compete against each other and are assessed by judges appointed by the town council as they each pass a specially erected pavilion, called, what else but the Sambadrome. The schools of dancers, of which there are hundreds, can be enormous numbering even thousands' strong. Each school comprises three sections, the musicians called ritmistas, the dancers called passistas and the floats carrying the glamorous ladies, mostly in skimpy costumes with beautiful head adornments.

FRED AND GINGER It was 100 years ago, in 1905, that Europe saw any form of Samba. The first form to invade Europe was called the Maxixe. It was featured in George Edward's stage production, *Lady Madcap*. A famous dance couple of the early 20th century, Vernon and Irene Castle, featured the dance in their shows. Vernon was a Briton who had emigrated to New York, where he and his American wife, Irene, became probably the leading dance couple of the era. However, the Maxixe, while related to the Samba, was not its full blooded ancestor. Signs of what was to come were apparent in the 1933 film *Flying Down to Rio*, which featured Fred Astaire and

Promotional poster for the 1933 film, *Flying down to Rio*, starring Fred Astaire and Ginger Rogers.

Ginger Rogers, dancing together for the first time. The film includes the Carioca, a dance with a Samba influence. Carioca is the name of a small river running through Rio, and Samba dancers often call themselves Cariocas. The real impact of Samba that helped to establish the music and dance came with the films of Carmen Miranda and with the world's Fair in New York, in 1939, where the Brazilian Government sent a large number of immensely popular Samba bands.

SAMBA VARIATIONS We say 'the dance' but by now you will realize that there are many variations, for example, there is a slow version known as the Baion and a fast version that is more like marching music. It is not surprising that there are so many forms of Samba and the music, when one considers not only the historical background but also the fact that the country is so large. Brazil is more than 34 times larger than (and has a population three times larger than) that of the UK, and excluding Alaska and Hawaii, it is larger than the USA in area.

THE HOLD AND DANCE FIGURES Most dancers prefer the Open Hold (see page 18) but some find a closer hold suits them better.

Samba music is in 2/4 time and, as with all Latin dances, it can be complex but for beginners there is no need to be concerned with the more intricate developments of the rhythms. All the figures described are built around a basis of two slow steps to each bar of music. When you have progressed a little more there will, as you might expect, be variations on this simple rhythm.

On Shrove Tuesday (or Mardi Gras) a magnificent parade passes through Rio de Janeiro – everyone dances joyfully and wears fantastic costumes and especially huge and flamboyant head dresses.

Carmen Miranda – famous for her truly flamboyant headdresses – and Hermes Pan performing the Samba in the 1941 film, *That Night in Rio*.

Left Pendulum

When you have the pattern of the figure clear in your mind, there is a 'bounce action' on the steps, which will improve your enjoyment of the dance. Start with both knees slightly bent, and on each beat of music straighten the legs and knees (though not stiffly) and then bend again. So over the four steps you will also have a pattern of bouncing: up, down, up down, up down, up down. This is a subtle movement and you should take care not to overdo it.

All this may look a little daunting but if you learn the figures step-by-step you should not find it very difficult. The characteristic bounce action can be added to all Samba figures in this book.

The steps here are described without turns but when comfortable with the pattern you can turn a little to the left throughout the figure.

	Count:	**Man's Steps**		**Lady's Steps**	
		M		**L**	
One	1	LEFT FOOT takes a medium step forwards, taking one beat of music.	1	RIGHT FOOT takes a medium step backwards, taking one beat of music.	
Two	2	RIGHT FOOT closes to left foot, putting a little pressure on right foot but retaining weight on the left foot and taking one beat of music.	2	LEFT FOOT closes to right foot, putting a little pressure on the left foot but retaining weight on the right foot and taking one beat of music.	
One	3	RIGHT FOOT takes a medium step backwards, taking one beat of music.	3	LEFT FOOT takes a medium step forwards, taking one beat of music.	
Two	4	LEFT FOOT closes to right foot, putting a little pressure on the left foot but retaining weight on the right foot and taking one beat of music.	4	RIGHT FOOT closes to left foot, putting a little pressure on right foot but retaining weight on the left foot and taking one beat of music.	

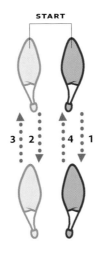

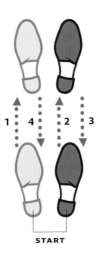

Link and Right Pendulum

Once you have become familiar with the foot patterns, try turning to the right slightly throughout the figure, together with the 'bounce action' described on page 154. Steps 3–6 comprise the Right Pendulum and can be repeated as often as you wish. When you have completed steps 1–6, steps 3 and 4 can be danced again, to allow you to follow this figure with another that commences with the man's left foot and the lady's right foot.

	Man's Steps		Lady's Steps
Count:	**M**		**L**
One 1	LEFT FOOT takes a step to the side, taking one beat of music.	1	RIGHT FOOT takes a step to the side, taking one beat of music.
Two 2	RIGHT FOOT closes to left foot, putting a little pressure on right foot but retaining weight on left foot and taking one beat of music.	2	LEFT FOOT closes to right foot, putting a little pressure on left foot but retaining weight on right foot and taking one beat of music.
One 3	RIGHT FOOT takes a step forwards, taking one beat of music.	3	LEFT FOOT takes a step backwards, taking one beat of music.
Two 4	LEFT FOOT closes to right foot, putting a little pressure on left foot but retaining weight on right foot and taking one beat of music.	4	RIGHT FOOT closes to left foot, putting a little pressure on right foot but retaining weight on left foot and taking one beat of music.
One 5	LEFT FOOT takes a step backwards, taking one beat of music.	5	RIGHT FOOT takes a step forwards, taking one beat of music.
Two 6	RIGHT FOOT closes to left foot, putting a little pressure on right foot but retaining weight on left foot and taking one beat of music.	6	LEFT FOOT closes to right foot, putting a little pressure on left foot but retaining weight on right foot and taking one beat of music.

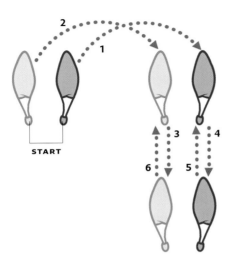

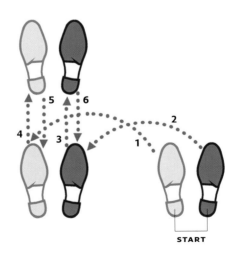

Left Pendulum

One

Two

One

1 **M** LEFT FOOT takes a step forwards.
L RIGHT FOOT takes a step backwards.
Takes one beat of music.

2 **M** RIGHT FOOT closes to left foot, retaining weight on left foot.
L LEFT FOOT closes to right foot, retaining weight on right foot.
Takes one beat of music.

3 **M** RIGHT FOOT takes a step backwards.
L LEFT FOOT takes a step forwards.
Takes one beat of music.

Link and Right Pendulum

One

Two

One

1 **M** LEFT FOOT takes a step to the side.
L RIGHT FOOT takes a step to the side.
Takes one beat of music.

2 **M** RIGHT FOOT closes to left foot, retaining weight on left foot.
L LEFT FOOT closes to right foot, retaining weight on right foot.
Takes one beat of music.

3 **M** RIGHT FOOT takes a step forwards.
L LEFT FOOT takes a step backwards.
Takes one beat of music.

Two

4 **M** LEFT FOOT closes to right foot, retaining weight on right foot.
L RIGHT FOOT closes to left foot, retaining weight on left foot.
Takes one beat of music.

Progressive Links

This movement is useful when you want to move around the room a little. Face the nearest wall and turn a little to the left until you are 'facing diagonally to wall', then dance the first four steps of the Link and Right Pendulum, as man and lady, and it will take you along a line generally parallel to wall.

The count for this is: side, close, step, close. The steps and thus the count can be repeated as often as you wish.

Two

4 **M** LEFT FOOT closes to right foot, retaining weight on right foot.
L RIGHT FOOT closes to left foot, retaining weight on left foot.
Takes one beat of music.

One

5 **M** LEFT FOOT takes a step backwards.
L RIGHT FOOT takes a step forwards.
Takes one beat of music.

Two

6 **M** RIGHT FOOT closes to left foot, retaining weight on left foot.
L LEFT FOOT closes to right foot, retaining weight on right foot.
Takes one beat of music.

Outside Pendulum

This figure gives a little variety to the pendulum action. It consists of the Link and Right Pendulum (see pages 156–9) with the addition of a contrary turn that allows for the lady to step to her left of her partner's body, that is, 'outside partner'. When you feel happy with this figure, you can add the bounce action (see page 154).

		Man's Steps		Lady's Steps
Count:		**M**		**L**
One	1	LEFT FOOT takes a step to the side.	1	RIGHT FOOT takes a step to the side.
Two	2	RIGHT FOOT closes to left foot, putting a little pressure on right foot but retaining weight on left foot.	2	LEFT FOOT closes to right foot, putting a little pressure on left foot but retaining weight on right foot.
One	3	RIGHT FOOT takes a step forwards, turning to left. This turn is a little unusual so make sure that you turn towards your left side.	3	LEFT FOOT takes a step backwards, turning to left. This turn is a little unusual so make sure that you turn towards your left side.
Two	4	LEFT FOOT closes to right foot, putting a little pressure on left foot but retaining weight on right foot, still turning left.	4	RIGHT FOOT closes to left foot, putting a little pressure on right foot but retaining weight on left foot, still turning left.
One	5	LEFT FOOT takes a step backwards, bringing partner forwards on your right side ('outside partner').	5	RIGHT FOOT takes a step forwards to your left of your partner ('outside partner').
Two	6	RIGHT FOOT closes to left foot, putting a little pressure on right foot but retaining weight on left foot.	6	LEFT FOOT closes to right foot, putting a little pressure on left foot but retaining weight on right foot.
One	7	RIGHT FOOT takes a step forwards to your left of your partner's feet ('outside partner'), starting to turn to the right.	7	LEFT FOOT takes a step backwards with partner stepping to your right side ('outside partner'), starting to turn to the right.
Two	8	LEFT FOOT closes to right foot, putting a little pressure on left foot but retaining weight on right foot and completing turn to right to finish facing your partner in normal hold.	8	RIGHT FOOT closes to left foot, putting a little pressure on right foot but retaining weight on left foot and completing turn to right to finish facing your partner in normal hold.

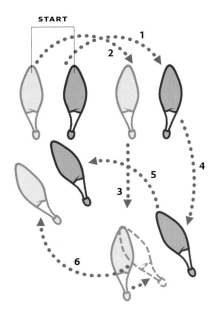

START

1

2

3

4

5

6

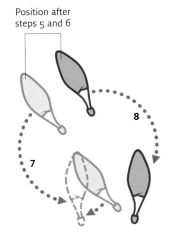

Position after
steps 5 and 6

7

8

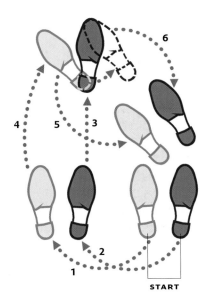

6

4

5

3

1

2

START

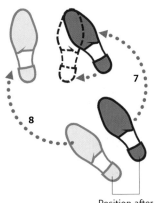

7

8

Position after
steps 5 and 6

Samba Whisks

This figure is fun and is a means of turning into the promenade position, where the man's left and the lady's right side pull away from each other so that their bodies make a V pattern when viewed from above. This allows them to step forwards together using the open side of the V, after step 4.

Steps 1–4 can be repeated several times before dancing steps 5 and 6.

	Man's Steps		Lady's Steps

Count:	**M**		**L**
One 1	LEFT FOOT takes a step to the side.	1	RIGHT FOOT takes a step to the side.
Two 2	RIGHT FOOT crosses loosely behind left foot, putting slight pressure on the toes of right foot. Give the lady a push with the heel of your right hand, but do not push forwards with the left hand. This should cause her to turn left and finish with her left side away from you.	2	LEFT FOOT crosses loosely behind right foot, putting slight pressure on the toes of left foot. Your partner will lead you to turn your body to your left and finish with your left side away from him, try not to resist him but go along with the guidance.
One 3	RIGHT FOOT takes a step to the side, pushing on partner's right hand with your left hand turning her to normal position to face you.	3	LEFT FOOT takes a step to the side, turning to face partner in normal position (partner should have led you into the position).
Two 4	LEFT FOOT crosses loosely behind right foot putting slight pressure on the toes of left foot. Increase the pressure of the right hand on the lady's back and push forwards a little with the left hand. These hand actions should cause the lady to turn her right side away from you.	4	RIGHT FOOT crosses loosely behind left foot, putting slight pressure on the toes of right foot. Your partner will push your right hand backwards. These hand actions should guide you to turn your right side away from the man.
One 5	LEFT FOOT takes a step to the side, turning your partner to face you, relaxing pressure with right hand and pulling left hand back slightly.	5	RIGHT FOOT takes a step to the side, turning to face partner. The pressure from the man's right hand has been relaxed.
Two 6	RIGHT FOOT closes to left foot, putting slight pressure on the toes of your right foot.	6	LEFT FOOT closes to right foot, putting slight pressure on the toes of your right foot.

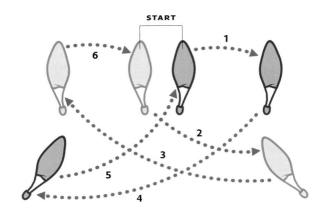

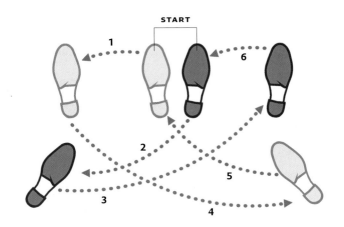

Outside Pendulum

One

Two

One

Two

1 **M** LEFT FOOT takes a step to the side.
L RIGHT FOOT takes a step to the side.

2 **M** RIGHT FOOT closes to left foot, retaining weight on left foot.
L LEFT FOOT closes to right foot, retaining weight on right foot.

3 **M** RIGHT FOOT takes a step forwards, turning to the left.
L LEFT FOOT takes a step backwards, turning to the left.

4 **M** LEFT FOOT closes to right foot, retaining weight on right foot.
L RIGHT FOOT closes to left foot, retaining weight on left foot. Both still turning left.

Samba Whisks

One

Two

One

1 **M** LEFT FOOT takes a step to the side.
L RIGHT FOOT takes a step to the side.

2 **M** RIGHT FOOT crosses loosely behind left foot. Gently push lady with right hand so she turns.
L LEFT FOOT crosses loosely behind right foot, turning to your left.

3 **M** RIGHT FOOT to the side, turning partner by pushing on her right hand with your left hand.
L LEFT FOOT to the side, turning to face partner.

One

Two

One

Two

5 **M** LEFT FOOT takes a step backwards, guiding lady to step 'outside partner'.
L RIGHT FOOT takes a step forwards, stepping 'outside partner'.

6 **M** RIGHT FOOT closes to left foot, retaining weight on left foot.
L LEFT FOOT closes to right foot, retaining weight on right foot.

7 **M** RIGHT FOOT takes a step forwards, 'outside partner', starting to turn to the right.
L LEFT FOOT takes a step backwards, starting to turn to the right.

8 **M** LEFT FOOT closes to right foot, completing turn to right.
L RIGHT FOOT closes to left foot, completing turn to right to finish facing partner.

Two

One

Two

4 **M** LEFT FOOT crosses loosely behind right foot. Increase pressure of right hand on lady's back.
L RIGHT FOOT crosses loosely behind left foot, turning to right side.

5 **M** LEFT FOOT to the side turning partner to face you, pulling your left hand back slightly.
L RIGHT FOOT to the side, turning to face partner.

6 **M** RIGHT FOOT closes to left foot putting slight pressure on right foot.
L LEFT FOOT closes to right foot, putting slight pressure on right foot.

Salsa

Robi Rosa ('Rico') and Magali Alvarado ('Rita') performing the Salsa from the 1988 film of the same name.

Currently Salsa is probably the most popular of the Cuban-based dances and, musically, it is a complicated blend of the historical Cuban dance forms such as Son, Danson, Guajira, Guaracha, Mambo, Cha Cha Cha, plus Colombian Cumbia, and Puerto Rican Bomba.

To this cocktail of rhythm has been added the drive and vitality of the American music scene with its jazz and rock traditions. A very heady mixture full of life and vitality is the result.

The Spanish word *salsa* means sauce but musicians think of it more as spice and this is just what you should have in mind when attempting the dance. The music first came to notice in the 1960s in the USA and perhaps the confirmation that it had arrived was the release of the film *Salsa* in 1988.

BODY ACTION This is a dance where body action is as important as movement, if not more so. The dances from Latin-America, and particularly those from the Caribbean, are complex with historical influences from the original natives, the Spanish invaders and

Members of the Eddie Torres Salsa Company demonstrate how to perform this energetic dance.

the multitude of African slaves that were imported into the countries. From the African slaves came the complex drum and rhythm instrument patterns, and also the erect carriage of the body that was essential for anyone who had to carry containers on their head. Stemming from this custom, the shoulders and head are kept still, so far as possible, in the steps of dances with a Caribbean history such as Salsa.

THE HOLD AND HIP ACTION For this dance use the Open Hold (see page 18).

Movement of the hips is common to many Latin dances with a Cuban/Caribbean history. It is described in some detail below. Much of the enjoyment and, indeed, the exercise benefits of these dances come from a fluid hip action.

Start with your feet a few inches apart and knees relaxed. Take the weight fully onto your flat left foot straightening the knee and letting the weight of your body settle onto your left hip, pushing it out sideways. If you have a fluid waist this will be easy, if not, this will assist you in achieving one. Now take the weight over the flat right foot. Straighten the right knee letting the weight of your body settle onto the right hip, pushing it out sideways. This settling of the weight over the supporting foot allows the hips to move sideways, and takes place on most steps where weight is transferred onto the foot. However, on a step that has two beats of music, the settling of the hip takes place on the second beat.

Vanessa L. Williams and Chayanne shimmy their way through a dance competition doing the Salsa, in the 1998 film, *Dance With Me*.

The Left Side Basic

Once you have practised these steps solo, you should try to master them with a partner. With a partner, when the man dances the Left Side Basic the lady dances the man's Right Side Basic (see pages 172–3) and vice versa.

The Left Side Basic can follow the Right Side Basic and vice versa, making a pattern of eight steps that can be repeated as often as you wish. Each step takes one beat of music.

	Count:	**Man's Steps**		**Lady's Steps**	
		M		**L**	
One	1	LEFT FOOT takes a small step to the side, straighten the leg and settle weight onto the foot so that your hips swing over to the left.	1	RIGHT FOOT takes a small step to the side, straighten the leg and settle weight onto the foot so that your hips swing over to the right.
Two	2	RIGHT FOOT closes half way towards left foot, straighten the leg and settle weight onto the foot so that hips swing over to right.	2	LEFT FOOT closes half way towards right foot, straighten the leg and settle weight onto the foot so that hips swing over to the left.
Three	3	LEFT FOOT takes a small step to the side, keeping the leg relaxed, without putting your full weight onto the foot.	3	RIGHT FOOT takes a small step to the side, keeping the leg relaxed, without putting your full weight onto the foot.
Four	4	LEFT LEG straightens and weight is settled fully over the foot so that hips swing over to the left and, at the same time, tap the toes of your right foot to the side of your left foot.	4	RIGHT LEG straightens and weight is settled fully over the foot so that hips swing over to the right and, at the same time, tap the toes of your left foot to the side of your right foot.

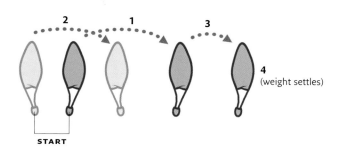

2   1   3

4
(weight settles)

START

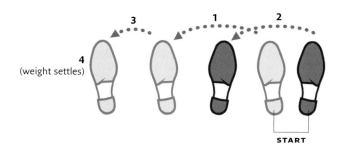

3   1   2

4
(weight settles)

START

The Right Side Basic

The Right Side Basic can follow the Left Side Basic and vice versa, making a pattern of eight steps that can be repeated as often as you wish.

	Man's Steps	Lady's Steps
Count:	**M**	**L**
One 1	RIGHT FOOT takes a small step to the side, straighten the leg and settle weight onto the foot so that your hips swing over to the right.	1 LEFT FOOT takes a small step to the side, straighten the leg and settle weight onto the foot so that your hips swing over to the left.
Two 2	LEFT FOOT closes half way towards right foot, straighten the leg and settle weight onto the foot so that hips swing over to the left.	2 RIGHT FOOT closes half way towards left foot, straighten the leg and settle weight onto the foot so that hips swing over to right.
Three 3	RIGHT FOOT takes a small step to the side, keeping the leg relaxed and without putting your full weight onto the foot.	3 LEFT FOOT takes a small step to the side, keeping the leg relaxed, and without putting your full weight onto the foot.
Four 4	RIGHT LEG straightens and weight is settled fully over the foot so that hips swing over to the right and, at the same time, tap the toes of your left foot to the side of your right foot.	4 LEFT LEG straightens and weight is settled fully over the foot so that hips swing over to the left and, at the same time, tap the toes of your right foot to the side of your left foot.

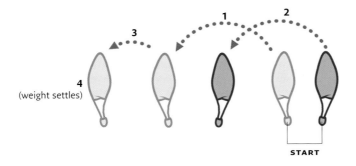

3

1

2

4
(weight settles)

START

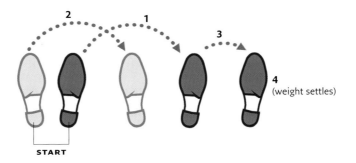

2

1

3

4
(weight settles)

START

Cucaracha Steps

One of the earliest Latin 'dances' to achieve real popularity was the Cucaracha (Spanish for cockroach). A dance with that name was featured in the Fred Astaire, Ginger Rogers film, *Flying Down to Rio*. How the name has come to be associated with this figure is not clear but it is a typical basic movement in Salsa and can also be found in some other Latin dances. In the following instructions each step takes one beat of music.

	Count:	**M**		**L**
One	1	LEFT FOOT takes a step to the side, pressing downwards into the floor but still retain some pressure on the right foot, while allowing the hips to swing to the left.	1	RIGHT FOOT takes a step to the side, pressing downwards into the floor but still retain some pressure on the left foot, while allowing the hips to swing to right.
Two	2	LEFT FOOT pushes off against the floor, taking the weight back fully onto the right foot, straighten right knee and allow the hips to swing to the right.	2	RIGHT FOOT pushes off against the floor, taking the weight back fully onto the left foot, straighten left knee and allow the hips to swing to the left.
Three	3	LEFT FOOT closes to right foot taking the weight onto left foot.	3	RIGHT FOOT closes to left foot taking the weight onto right foot.
Four	4	RIGHT FOOT lifts just off the floor with a flick action.	4	LEFT FOOT lifts just off the floor with a flick action.
One	5	RIGHT FOOT takes a step to the side, pressing downwards into the floor but still retain some pressure on the left foot, while allowing the hips to swing to right.	5	LEFT FOOT takes a step to the side, pressing downwards into the floor but still retain some pressure on the right foot, while allowing the hips to swing to left.
Two	6	RIGHT FOOT pushes off against the floor, taking the weight back fully onto the left foot, straighten left knee and allow the hips to swing to the left.	6	LEFT FOOT pushes off against the floor, taking weight back fully onto the right foot, straighten right knee and allow the hips to swing to the right.
Three	7	RIGHT FOOT closes to left foot, taking the weight onto right foot.	7	LEFT FOOT closes to right foot, taking the weight onto left foot.
Four	8	LEFT FOOT lifts just off the floor with a flick action.	8	RIGHT FOOT lifts just off the floor with a flick action.

Man's Steps   **Lady's Steps**

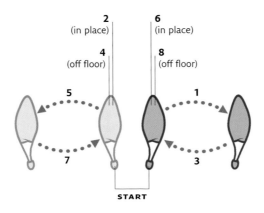

2
(in place)

6
(in place)

4
(off floor)

8
(off floor)

5

1

7

3

START

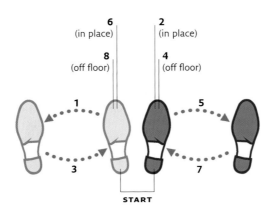

6
(in place)

2
(in place)

8
(off floor)

4
(off floor)

1

5

3

7

START

The Left Side Basic

One    *Two*    *Three*    *Four*

1   **M** LEFT FOOT to side, leg straightens, weight on foot, swing hips to left.
  L RIGHT FOOT to side, leg straightens, weight on foot, swing hips to right.

2   **M** RIGHT FOOT closes towards left foot, swing hips to the right.
  L LEFT FOOT closes towards right foot, leg straightens, swing hips to the left.

3   **M** LEFT FOOT to the side, without putting full weight onto the foot.
  L RIGHT FOOT to the side, without putting full weight onto the foot.

4   **M** LEFT LEG straightens, swing hips to the left and tap right toes.
  L RIGHT LEG straightens, swing hips to the right and tap left toes.

Cucaracha Steps

One    *Two*    *Three*    *Four*

1   **M** LEFT FOOT to the side, retain pressure on right foot, swing hips to left.
  L RIGHT FOOT to the side, retain some pressure on left foot, swing hips to right.

2   **M** LEFT FOOT pushes off against the floor, weight onto right foot, swing hips to right.
  L RIGHT FOOT pushes off against the floor, weight onto left foot, hips to left.

3   **M** LEFT FOOT closes to right foot, taking the weight onto left foot.
  L RIGHT FOOT closes to left foot, taking the weight onto right foot.

4   **M** RIGHT FOOT lifts just off the floor with a flick action.
  L LEFT FOOT lifts just off the floor with a flick action.

The Right Side Basic

One

Two

Three

Four

 1 M RIGHT FOOT to side, leg straightens, weight on foot, swing hips to right.
L LEFT FOOT to side, leg straightens, weight on foot, swing hips to left.

2 M LEFT FOOT closes towards right foot, swing hips to the left.
L RIGHT FOOT closes towards left foot, leg straightens, swing hips to the right.

3 M RIGHT FOOT to the side, without putting full weight onto the foot.
L LEFT FOOT to the side, without putting full weight onto the foot.

4 M RIGHT LEG straightens, swing hips to the right and tap left toes.
L LEFT LEG straightens, swing hips to the left and tap right toes.

One

Two

Three

Four

5 M RIGHT FOOT to the side, retain pressure on left foot, swing hips to right.
L LEFT FOOT to the side, retain pressure on right foot, swing hips to left.

6 M RIGHT FOOT pushes off against the floor, weight onto left foot, hips to left.
L LEFT FOOT pushes off against floor, weight onto right foot, swing hips to right.

7 M RIGHT FOOT closes to left foot, taking the weight onto right foot.
L LEFT FOOT closes to right foot, taking the weight onto left foot.

8 M LEFT FOOT lifts just off the floor with a flick action.
L RIGHT FOOT lifts just off the floor with a flick action.

Forwards and Backwards Basics

This figure can be danced after the Right Side Basic or the Cucaracha Steps (see pages 172–7).

		Man's Steps		Lady's Steps
Count:		**M**		**L**
One	1	LEFT FOOT takes a step forwards, settling hips to the left as the weight is taken onto the foot.	1	RIGHT FOOT takes a step backwards, settling hips to the right as the weight is taken onto the foot.
Two	2	RIGHT FOOT remains in place, settling hips to the right as the weight is taken backwards onto the foot.	2	LEFT FOOT remains in place, settling hips to the left as the weight is taken forwards onto the foot.
Three	3	LEFT FOOT closes to right foot with light pressure on the floor.	3	RIGHT FOOT closes to left foot with light pressure on the floor.
Four	4	LEFT FOOT takes the weight, at the same time, lift the right heel just off the floor.	4	RIGHT FOOT takes the weight, at the same time, lift the left heel just off the floor.
One	5	RIGHT FOOT takes a step backwards, settling hips to the right as the weight is taken onto the foot.	5	LEFT FOOT takes a step forwards, settling hips to the left as the weight is taken onto the foot.
Two	6	LEFT FOOT remains in place, settling hips to the left as the weight is taken forwards onto the foot.	6	RIGHT FOOT remains in place, settling hips to the right as the weight is taken backwards onto the foot.
Three	7	RIGHT FOOT closes to left foot with light pressure on the floor.	7	LEFT FOOT closes to right foot with light pressure on the floor.
Four	8	RIGHT FOOT takes the full weight, at same time, lift the left heel just off the floor.	8	LEFT FOOT takes the full weight, at same time, lift the right heel just off the floor.

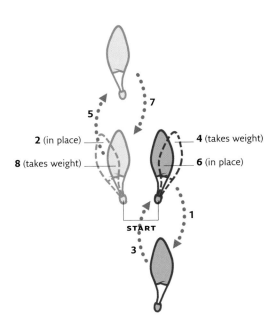

2 (in place)

8 (takes weight)

4 (takes weight)

6 (in place)

5

7

1

3

START

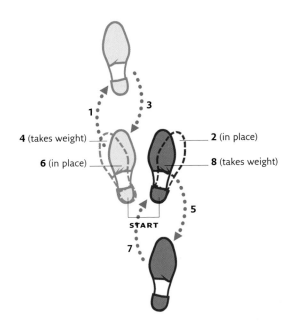

4 (takes weight)

6 (in place)

2 (in place)

8 (takes weight)

1

3

5

7

START

Left and Right Breaks

This group can follow the Right Side Basic, Cucaracha Steps, and Forwards and Backwards Basics (see pages 172–9).

	Count:	**Man's Steps** M		**Lady's Steps** L
One	1	LEFT FOOT takes a small step to the side, turn a little to the left, lower your left hand and push the lady's hand back slightly causing her to turn to her right.	1	RIGHT FOOT takes a small step to the side, lower your right hand and turn a little to the right, as a result of pressure on your hand from your partner.
Two	2	RIGHT FOOT remains in place but the weight is taken forwards onto it. Pull your left hand back a little, leading the lady to face you.	2	LEFT FOOT remains in place but the weight is taken forwards onto it, turning left to face your partner.
Three	3	LEFT FOOT closes to right foot with light pressure on the floor.	3	RIGHT FOOT closes to left foot with light pressure on the floor.
Four	4	LEFT FOOT takes the weight onto it, at the same time, lift the right heel just off the floor.	4	RIGHT FOOT takes the weight onto it, at the same time, lift the left heel just off the floor.
One	5	RIGHT FOOT takes a small step to the side, turn a little to the right and push on the lady's side with your right hand so as to guide her to turn to her left and then release hold with your right hand.	5	LEFT FOOT takes a small step to the side, turning left and causing the left side your of body to move away from your partner.
Two	6	LEFT FOOT remains in place but the weight is taken forwards onto it, leading the lady to face you.	6	RIGHT FOOT remains in place but weight is taken forwards onto it, turning to your right to face your partner.
Three	7	RIGHT FOOT closes to left foot with light pressure on the floor, turning to the left, guiding the lady to face you and regaining hold of her with your right hand.	7	LEFT FOOT closes to right foot with light pressure on the floor, now facing your partner.
Four	8	RIGHT FOOT takes the weight onto it, at the same time, lift the left heel just off the floor.	8	LEFT FOOT takes the weight onto it, at the same time, lift the right heel just off the floor.

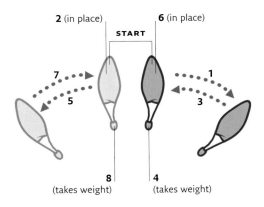

2 (in place)   **6** (in place)

START

7   5   1   3

8   **4**
(takes weight)   (takes weight)

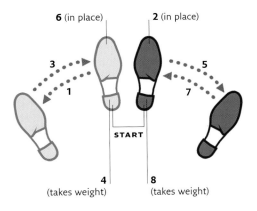

6 (in place)   **2** (in place)

3   1   5   7

START

4   **8**
(takes weight)   (takes weight)

Forwards and Backwards Basics

One   *Two*   *Three*   *Four*

1 **M** LEFT FOOT forwards, hips to the left as weight is taken onto the foot.
L RIGHT FOOT backwards, hips to the right as weight is taken onto the foot.

2 **M** RIGHT FOOT remains in place, takes the weight onto it, hips to the right.
L LEFT FOOT remains in place, takes the weight onto it, hips to the left.

3 **M** LEFT FOOT closes to right foot with light pressure on the floor.
L RIGHT FOOT closes to left foot with light pressure on the floor.

4 **M** LEFT FOOT takes the weight onto it, lift the right heel just off the floor.
L RIGHT FOOT takes the weight onto it, lift the left heel just off the floor.

Left and Right Breaks

One   *Two*   *Three*   *Four*

1 **M** LEFT FOOT to side, turn left, push the lady's hand back slightly causing her to turn to her right.
L RIGHT FOOT to side, lower right hand and turn a little to the right.

2 **M** RIGHT FOOT remains in place but weight is taken forwards onto it.
L LEFT FOOT remains in place but weight is taken onto it, turning left to face partner.

3 **M** LEFT FOOT closes to right foot with light pressure on the floor.
L RIGHT FOOT closes to left foot with light pressure on the floor.

4 **M** LEFT FOOT takes the weight onto it, at the same time, lift the right heel just off the floor.
L RIGHT FOOT takes the weight onto it, lift the left heel just off the floor.

One	*Two*	*Three*	*Four*

5 **M** RIGHT FOOT backwards, hips to the right as weight is taken onto the foot.
L LEFT FOOT forwards, hips to the left as weight is taken onto the foot.

6 **M** LEFT FOOT remains in place, takes the weight onto it, hips to the left.
L RIGHT FOOT remains in place, takes the weight onto it, hips to the right.

7 **M** RIGHT FOOT closes to left foot with light pressure on the floor.
L LEFT FOOT closes to right foot with light pressure on the floor.

8 **M** RIGHT FOOT takes the weight onto it, lift the left heel just off the floor.
L LEFT FOOT takes the weight onto it, lift the right heel just off the floor.

One	*Two*	*Three*	*Four*

5 **M** RIGHT FOOT to side, turn to the right, guiding the lady to turn left and let go with your right hand.
L LEFT FOOT to the side, turning left and moving away from your partner.

6 **M** LEFT FOOT remains in place but weight is taken forwards onto it.
L RIGHT FOOT remains in place but weight is taken onto it, turning right to face your partner.

7 **M** RIGHT FOOT closes to left foot, turning left and guiding lady with right hand to face you.
L LEFT FOOT closes to right foot, now facing your partner.

8 **M** RIGHT FOOT takes the weight onto it and lift the left heel just off the floor.
L LEFT FOOT takes the weight back onto it and lift the right heel just off the floor.

Outside Breaks

This figure follows Cucaracha Steps or Forwards and Backwards Basics (see pages 174–9). It can be repeated and benefits from doing so. When you are comfortable with this figure you might care to try to increase the lady's turns.

		Man's Steps		Lady's Steps
Count:		**M**		**L**
One	1	LEFT FOOT takes a small step forwards and across the body, turning to the right about 45–90 degrees as you step to your right of the lady's feet.	1	RIGHT FOOT takes a small step backwards, turning to the right about 45–90 degrees, allowing the man to step to your left side.
Two	2	RIGHT FOOT remains in place and weight is taken backwards onto it, starting to turn to the left.	2	LEFT FOOT remains in place and weight is transferred forwards onto it, starting to turn to the left.
Three	3	LEFT FOOT to the side of right foot, putting only part weight on foot, completing the turn to the left so as to face your partner again.	3	RIGHT FOOT to the side of left foot, putting only part weight onto foot, completing the turn to the left so as to face your partner again.
Four	4	LEFT FOOT remains in place and weight is taken fully onto it.	4	RIGHT FOOT remains in place and weight is taken fully onto it.
One	5	RIGHT FOOT takes a small step forwards and across the body, turning to the left about 45–90 degrees as you step to your left of the lady's feet.	5	LEFT FOOT takes a small step backwards, turning to the left about 45–90 degrees, allowing the man to step to your right side.
Two	6	LEFT FOOT remains in place and weight is taken backwards onto it, starting to turn to the right.	6	RIGHT FOOT remains in place and weight is taken forwards onto it, starting to turn to the right.
Three	7	RIGHT FOOT to the side of left foot, putting only part weight on foot, completing the turn to the right to face partner again.	7	LEFT FOOT to the side of right foot, putting only part weight on foot, completing the turn to the right to face partner again.
Four	8	RIGHT FOOT remains in place and weight taken fully onto it.	8	LEFT FOOT remains in place and weight taken fully onto it.

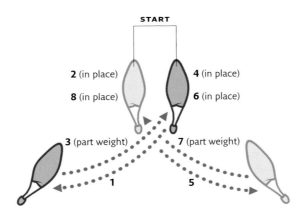

START

2 (in place)   **4** (in place)

8 (in place)   **6** (in place)

3 (part weight)   **7** (part weight)

1   5

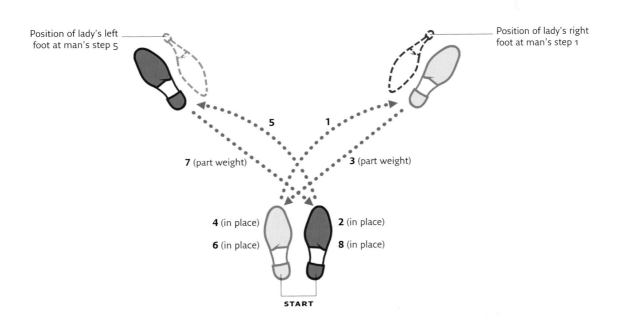

Position of lady's left
foot at man's step 5

Position of lady's right
foot at man's step 1

5   1

7 (part weight)   **3** (part weight)

4 (in place)   **2** (in place)

6 (in place)   **8** (in place)

START

Man and Lady Twirls

The figure starts after the Cucaracha Steps, Forwards and Backwards Basics or Outside Breaks (see pages 174–9, 184–5). Try to imagine the sequence. The man releases the lady from his right hand and guides her into a strong turn to the left, under his left and her right hand, for the first four beats of music. On the second four beats, she continues to turn but it is not such a strong turn. At the end of the second four beats, partners face each other again. The man makes a little turn, first to the right and then to the left, on the first four beats, he then makes a strong turn to the left under the raised hands, on the second four beats.

	Man's Steps		Lady's Steps

Count:	**M**		**L**
One 1	LEFT FOOT takes a small step forwards and across the body, turning slightly right. Release hold of the lady from your right hand, raise your left hand up over her head to form an arch and start turning her to the left by making an anticlockwise rotation of the left hand. Do not grip the lady's hand too firmly.	1	RIGHT FOOT takes a small step to the side on the ball of your foot, turning strongly to the left. The man will raise his left and your right hand to create an arch, under which first you and then he will turn. Allow your right hand to turn in the man's left hand. To turn sufficiently swivel on the balls of the feet.
Two 2	RIGHT FOOT closes near to left foot turning a little to the left, still turning the lady to her left.	2	LEFT FOOT closes to right foot, still turning strongly to the left.
Three-four 3	LEFT FOOT marks time drawing your left and the lady's right hand a little towards you, preparing for your turn. The step takes twice as long as the previous two steps.	3	RIGHT FOOT marks time, continuing the strong turn to the left.
One 4	RIGHT FOOT marks time on the ball of the foot, starting to turn to the left under the arch. To turn sufficiently, swivel on the right foot.	4	LEFT FOOT marks time, continuing to turn slightly to the left, allowing the man to start his turn to the left under the arch.
Two 5	LEFT FOOT marks time, continue turning strongly to the left, swivelling on the ball of your foot.	5	RIGHT FOOT marks time, the man is turning under the arch. You should now be facing your partner's back.
Three-four 6	RIGHT FOOT marks time, completing the turn to the left, lower your left hand and regain normal position.	6	LEFT FOOT marks time, lower your right hand and regain normal hold.

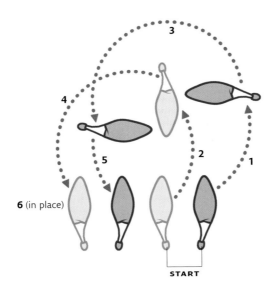

6 (in place)

3

4

5

2

1

START

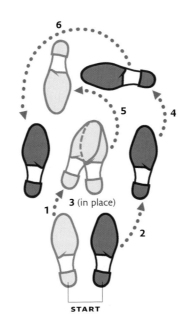

6

5

4

1

3 (in place)

2

START

Outside Breaks

One

Two

Three

Four

1 **M** LEFT FOOT forwards, turning right as you step 'outside partner'.
L RIGHT FOOT backwards, turning right, allowing the man to step to your left side.

2 **M** RIGHT FOOT remains in place, weight is taken onto it, turning left.
L LEFT FOOT remains in place and weight is taken onto it, turning to the left.

3 **M** LEFT FOOT to side of right foot with part weight on foot.
L RIGHT FOOT to side of left foot with part weight on foot.
Both turn to face partner.

4 **M** LEFT FOOT remains in place and weight is taken fully onto it.
L RIGHT FOOT remains in place and weight is taken fully onto it.

Taking a Turn

The essence of Salsa is the turning of partners with respect to each other and these turns can be very intricate. If you are fortunate enough to be practising with a partner, try the Man and Lady Twirls (right), which consists of a fairly simple group of turning steps.

Some couples find it easier to make the turns if the man bends his second finger of his left hand down from the remaining fingers and the lady loosely holds the finger and uses it as a pivot for the turns.

Man and Lady Twirls

One

Two

1 **M** LEFT FOOT forwards and across, turn slightly to right, raise hand and start to turn the lady left.
L RIGHT FOOT to side, turn strongly to the left under arch.

2 **M** RIGHT FOOT closes near to left foot turning a little to the left, still turning the lady to her left.
L LEFT FOOT closes to right foot, still turning strongly to the left.

One	Two	Three	Four

5 **M** RIGHT FOOT forwards and across the body, turning left as you step 'outside partner'.
  L LEFT FOOT backwards, turning to the left, as man steps to your right.

6 **M** LEFT FOOT remains in place, weight is taken onto it, turning to right.
  L RIGHT FOOT remains in place, weight is taken onto it, turning to right.

7 **M** RIGHT FOOT to side of left foot with part weight on foot.
  L LEFT FOOT to side of right foot with part weight on foot.
  Both turn to face partner.

8 **M** RIGHT FOOT remains in place and weight taken fully onto it.
  L LEFT FOOT remains in place and weight taken fully onto it.

Three-four	One	Two	Three-four

3 **M** LEFT FOOT marks time, drawing your left and the lady's right hand a little towards you.
  L RIGHT FOOT marks time, still turning strongly to the left.

4 **M** RIGHT FOOT marks time on ball of foot, starting strong turn to the left under the arch formed.
  L LEFT FOOT marks time, still turning slightly to the left.

5 **M** LEFT FOOT marks time, still turning strongly to the left and swivelling on ball of foot.
  L RIGHT FOOT marks time, partner is still turning under the arch.

6 **M** RIGHT FOOT marks time, completing the turn to the left, lower left hand, regain normal position.
  L LEFT FOOT marks time, lower right hand and regain normal hold.

Tango

Dancers from the 2002 film *Assassination Tango* capture the seductive power of the dance.

The Tango has a very special character all of its own.
There are erudite arguments about its true origins
and one French academic claimed that he could trace
the dance back to the days of Ancient Greece.

Generally, the Tango is believed to have originated in Argentina and especially Buenos Aires. In the early years of the 20th century it was danced solo by prostitutes to entice men into the bordellos. It developed into a dance for couples with, at its more advanced levels, intricate movements where partners' legs became intertwined and with very close body contact. In those early years men could often be seen in the back streets of Argentine towns, practising the complicated figures in order to impress the ladies with their dancing prowess.

STACCATO RHYTHM As with all dances, Tango has changed over the years. The basic rhythm of the music has changed from that of the Habanera to Milonga. In the mid-1930s a German dancer, Freddie Camp, revolutionized the dance with a more vigorous approach to the rhythm that has become known as staccato. In recent years, this has been somewhat overdone but does not affect those learning the dance at the early stages.

The character of the dance is unique. It does not flow in the same way as most body-contact dances with each step blending into the next and with a flow of body movement. In Tango each step is taken much as in walking. There are three major differences. One: the hold is much more compact and the man reaches further around his partner with his right hand and arm. Two: the feet are picked up and placed into position rather than skimming the floor. Three: the pattern of walking steps follows a slight curve to the left so that when the man steps forwards with his left foot the step is taken slightly across the body. If dancers keep in mind the movement of any member of the cat family when stalking prey that will go a long way to achieving the correct character for the dance.

In many ways the Tango is an easy dance, but to achieve feeling for the dance the music is vital. It is important to listen to the music, the tune as well as the rhythm. The music is in 2/4 and has a more authentic feeling when it is in a minor key.

BASIC TANGO HOLD The couple stand in very close contact, with the lady's right hip roughly central on the man's body. The man reaches further around the lady with his right hand and arm, and his left hand is drawn closer to the head than in the other ballroom dances. The lady moves her left hand further around the man's right arm.

Heart-throb Rudolph Valentino dancing the Tango with Beatrice Dominguez in the 1921 film, *The Four Horsemen of the Apocalypse*.

A more recent demonstration of the Tango. This scene comes from the 1992 film, *Scent of a Woman*, in which Al Pacino dances with Gabrielle Anwar.

The Walks into the Progressive Side Step

In this figure steps 1–2 are known as the Walks and steps 3–6 are the Progressive Side Step. The complete figure makes a slight curve to the left.

Man's Steps

Start facing the nearest wall, then twist your body a little to the left bringing your right shoulder forwards.

Lady's Steps

Start backing the nearest wall, then twist your body a little to the left bringing your left shoulder backwards.

Count:		M		L
Slow	1	LEFT FOOT takes a step forwards and slightly across the line of the right foot, with the left foot turned very slightly out, that is, pointing a little to the left, taking one beat of music.	1	RIGHT FOOT takes a step backwards and slightly across the line of the left foot, with the right foot turned in very slightly, that is, pointing a little to the left, taking one beat of music.
Slow	2	RIGHT FOOT takes a step forwards with the foot pointing a little to the left, taking one beat of music.	2	LEFT FOOT takes a step backwards with the foot pointing a little to the left, taking one beat of music.
Quick	3	LEFT FOOT takes a step forwards and slightly across the line of the right foot with the left foot turned very slightly out, that is, pointing a little to the left, taking half a beat of music.	3	RIGHT FOOT takes a step backwards and slightly across the line of the left foot with the right foot turned very slightly in, that is, pointing a little to the left, taking half a beat of music.
Quick	4	RIGHT FOOT takes a small step to the side and slightly back of left foot, taking half a beat of music.	4	LEFT FOOT takes a small step to the side and slightly forwards of right foot, with foot pointing a little to the left, taking half a beat of music.
Slow	5	LEFT FOOT takes a step forwards and slightly across the line of the right foot with the left foot turned very slightly out, that is, pointing a little to the left, taking one beat of music.	5	RIGHT FOOT takes a step backwards and slightly across the line of the left foot, with the right foot turned very slightly in, that is, pointing a little to the left, taking one beat of music.
Slow	6	RIGHT FOOT takes a step forwards with the foot pointing a little to the left, taking one beat of music.	6	LEFT FOOT takes a step backwards, with the foot pointing a little to the left, taking one beat of music.

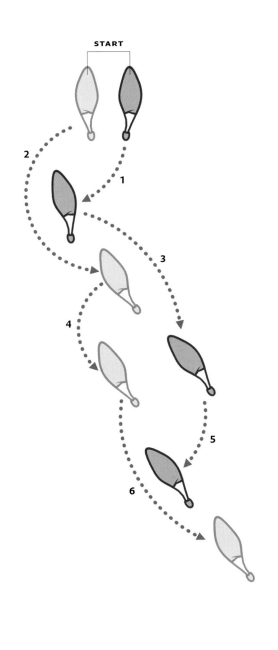

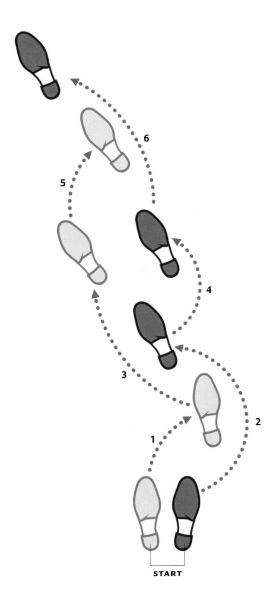

Progressive Link into Promenade

This figure can follow The Walks into the Progressive Side Step (see pages 194–5), either after step 2 or step 6, and is used when you and your partner want to turn into promenade position. This position is reached by the use of the Progressive Link (steps 1–2 below).

Man's Steps

Start by 'facing diagonally to wall' in normal close Tango hold. By step 2 you should be 'facing diagonally to wall' in promenade position.

Lady's Steps

Start by 'backing diagonally to wall' in normal close Tango hold. By step 2 you should be 'facing diagonally to centre' in promenade position.

Count:		**M**		**L**
Quick	1	LEFT FOOT takes a step forwards and slightly across the line of the right foot with the left foot pointing a little to the left.	1	RIGHT FOOT takes a step backwards and slightly across the line of the left foot with the right foot pointing a little to the left.
Quick	2	RIGHT FOOT takes a small step to side and slightly behind the line of left foot. Press firmly on the lady's back with heel of right hand to guide her to turn into promenade position.	2	LEFT FOOT takes a small step to side and slightly behind the line of right foot, turning to the right into promenade position with right side 25 cm (1 ft) or so away from partner.
Slow	3	LEFT FOOT takes a step to the side along a line parallel to the wall in promenade position, with left foot pointing diagonally to wall.	3	RIGHT FOOT takes a step to the side along a line parallel to the wall in promenade position, with right foot pointing diagonally to centre.
Quick	4	RIGHT FOOT steps across left foot, moving foot along a line parallel to the wall, still in promenade position, with foot pointing diagonally to wall.	4	LEFT FOOT steps across right foot, moving foot along a line parallel to the wall, in promenade position, with left foot pointing diagonally to centre.
Quick	5	LEFT FOOT takes a step to the side along a line parallel to the wall, with left foot pointing diagonally to wall, and turning partner to face you.	5	RIGHT FOOT takes a step to the side along a line parallel to the wall, turning to the left to face the man and 'backing diagonally to wall'.
Slow	6	RIGHT FOOT closes to left foot, closing right toe to left instep.	6	LEFT FOOT closes to right foot, closing left instep to right toe.

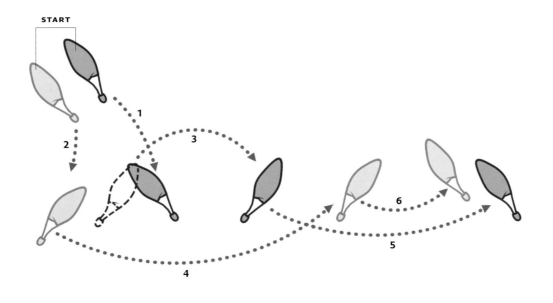

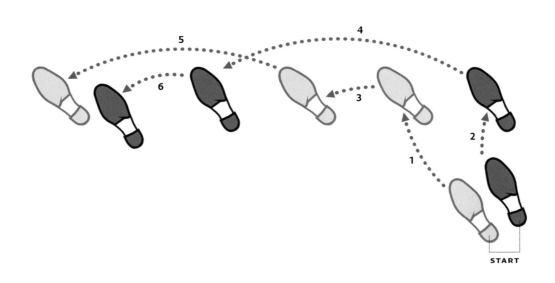

The Walks into the Progressive Side Step

Slow

1 **M** LEFT FOOT forwards and slightly across the line of the right foot.
L RIGHT FOOT backwards and slightly across the line of the left foot.
Takes one beat of music.

Slow

2 **M** RIGHT FOOT forwards with the foot pointing a little to the left.
L LEFT FOOT backwards with foot pointing a little to the left.
Takes one beat of music.

Quick

3 **M** LEFT FOOT forwards and across the line of the right foot.
L RIGHT FOOT backwards and slightly across the line of the left foot.
Takes half a beat of music.

Progressive Link into Promenade

Quick

1 **M** LEFT FOOT forwards and slightly across line of right foot.
L RIGHT FOOT backwards and slightly across line of the left foot.

Quick

2 **M** RIGHT FOOT to side behind line of left foot, pressing firmly on lady's back with right hand.
L LEFT FOOT a small step to side and turning into promenade position.

Slow

3 **M** LEFT FOOT to side along a line parallel to the wall in promenade position.
L RIGHT FOOT to side along a line parallel to the wall, in promenade position.

Quick

Slow

Slow

4 **M** RIGHT FOOT a small step to the side and slightly back of left foot.
   L LEFT FOOT to the side and slightly forwards of right foot.
   Takes half a beat of music.

5 **M** LEFT FOOT forwards and slightly across the line of the right foot.
   L RIGHT FOOT backwards and slightly across the line of the left foot.
   Takes one beat of music.

6 **M** RIGHT FOOT forwards with the foot pointing a little to the left.
   L LEFT FOOT backwards with foot pointing a little to the left.
   Takes one beat of music.

Quick

Quick

Slow

4 **M** RIGHT FOOT steps across left foot along a line parallel to the wall.
   L LEFT FOOT steps across right foot along a line parallel to the wall.

5 **M** LEFT FOOT to side along a line parallel to the wall, turning lady to face you.
   L RIGHT FOOT to side along a line parallel to the wall, turning to the left to face partner.

6 **M** RIGHT FOOT closes to left foot, closing right toe to left instep.
   L LEFT FOOT closes to right foot, closing left instep to right toe. This is 'tango closed' position.

Open Promenade

This figure is very similar to the Promenade but has a different form of ending. Like the Promenade you need to be in the promenade position, using the Progressive Link (see pages 196–7) in order to start. The figure can be followed by The Walks (see pages 194–5), with the man and the lady coming in line with one another on the first step, that is, with the man's left foot following the line of the lady's right foot. Alternatively, dance the Rock on Left Foot (see pages 202–5) after this figure.

	Count:	**Man's Steps**		**Lady's Steps**
		M		**L**
Slow	1	LEFT FOOT takes a step to the side along a line parallel to the wall in promenade position, with the left foot pointing diagonally to wall.	1	RIGHT FOOT takes a step to the side along a line parallel to the wall, in promenade position, with the right foot pointing diagonally to centre.
Quick	2	RIGHT FOOT steps across left foot moving the foot along a line parallel to wall, still in promenade position with right foot pointing diagonally to wall.	2	LEFT FOOT steps across right foot moving foot along a line parallel to wall, in promenade position, with left foot pointing diagonally to centre.
Quick	3	LEFT FOOT takes a step to the side along a line parallel to the wall, with left foot pointing diagonally to wall, and turning your partner to face you.	3	RIGHT FOOT takes a step to the side along a line parallel to the wall, turning to the left to face your partner.
Slow	4	RIGHT FOOT takes a step forwards across your body passing to your left of your partner's body – 'outside partner'. Try to maintain body contact throughout the step.	4	LEFT FOOT takes a step backwards, with partner stepping to the right side of your body. Try to maintain body contact as the step is taken.

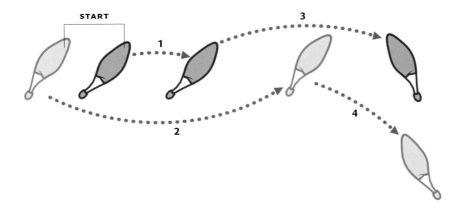

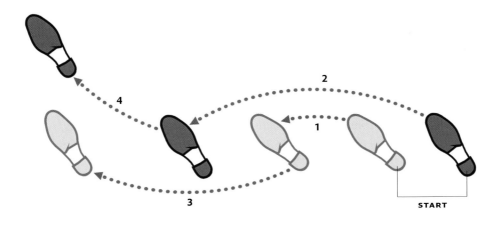

Rock on Left Foot (with Closed Ending)

On the first three steps of this group the couple do not move their feet, but as the name suggests, merely rock their weight backwards and forwards from foot to foot. This figure should be danced after the Open Promenade (see pages 200–1).

	Man's Steps	Lady's Steps

Count:	**M**		**L**
Quick **1**	TRANSFER WEIGHT backwards onto left foot with partner on your right side.	**1**	TRANSFER WEIGHT forwards onto right foot with partner on your right side.
Quick **2**	TRANSFER WEIGHT forwards onto right foot with partner still on your right side.	**2**	TRANSFER WEIGHT backwards onto left foot with partner still on your right side.
Slow **3**	TRANSFER WEIGHT backwards onto left foot with partner still on your right side.	**3**	TRANSFER WEIGHT forwards onto right foot with partner still on your right side.
Quick **4**	RIGHT FOOT takes a step backwards, beginning to turn to left and bringing partner into line so that her left foot follows the line of your right foot.	**4**	LEFT FOOT takes a step forwards, beginning to turn to left and moving into line with partner.
Quick **5**	LEFT FOOT takes a small step to the side, still turning to the left.	**5**	RIGHT FOOT takes a step to the side, still turning to the left.
Slow **6**	RIGHT FOOT closes to left foot with right toe closing to left instep (the typical Tango closed position).	**6**	LEFT FOOT closes to right foot with left instep closing to right toe (the typical Tango closed position).

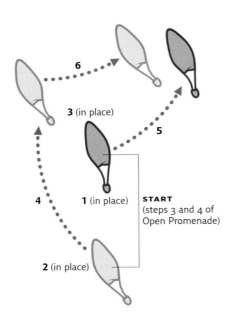

6

3 (in place)

5

4

1 (in place)

START
(steps 3 and 4 of
Open Promenade)

2 (in place)

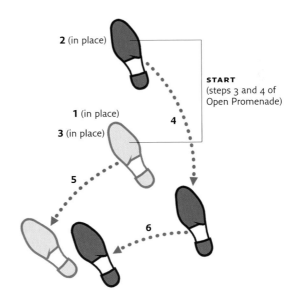

2 (in place)

START
(steps 3 and 4 of
Open Promenade)

1 (in place)

3 (in place)

4

5

6

Open Promenade

Slow

Quick

Quick

1 **M** LEFT FOOT takes a step to the side along a line parallel to the wall.
L RIGHT FOOT takes a step to the side along a line parallel to the wall.

2 **M** RIGHT FOOT steps across left foot along a line parallel to the wall.
L LEFT FOOT steps across right foot along a line parallel to the wall.

3 **M** LEFT FOOT to side along a line parallel to the wall, turning lady to face you.
L RIGHT FOOT to side along a line parallel to the wall, turning to the left to face partner.

Rock on Left Foot (with Closed Ending)

Quick

Quick

Slow

1 **M** TRANSFER WEIGHT backwards onto left foot, lady on your right side.
L TRANSFER WEIGHT forwards onto right foot, with the man on your right side.

2 **M** TRANSFER WEIGHT forwards onto right foot, lady still on right side.
L TRANSFER WEIGHT backwards onto left foot, with the man still on your right side.

3 **M** TRANSFER WEIGHT backwards onto left foot, lady still on right side.
L TRANSFER WEIGHT forwards onto right foot, with the man still on your right side.

Slow

4 **M** RIGHT FOOT forwards across your body stepping 'outside partner'.
L LEFT FOOT backwards with partner stepping to your right.

In many ways the Tango is an easy dance but to achieve feeling for the dance, the music is vital. It is important to listen to the tune as well as the rhythm.

Quick

4 **M** RIGHT FOOT backwards, beginning to turn to left.
L LEFT FOOT forwards, beginning to turn to left and moving into line with partner.

Quick

5 **M** LEFT FOOT takes a small step to the side, still turning to the left.
L RIGHT FOOT takes a small step to the side, still turning to the left.

Slow

6 **M** RIGHT FOOT closes to left foot with right toe closing to left instep.
L LEFT FOOT closes to right foot with left instep closing to right toe.

Rumba

Grupo AfroCuba de Matanzas performing
the Rumba in Cuba in 1995.

Rumba is the common name for the dance of Cuba but it is a misnomer because there is no one dance of Cuba, there are many. It has been used for many years as a general name covering all Cuban dances.

As with all Caribbean music and dances, the major impact came from African slaves in the three and a half centuries following the first discovery of America and the annexation of Cuba for Spain by Christopher Columbus in 1492. The Spaniards established sugar plantations in Cuba, which needed a great many workers to produce the sugar. The native Cubans were sparse in numbers and the diseases carried by the conquerors, such as measles, were devastating to the native population who had never before been exposed to these diseases. The death toll was immense and labour was needed. It was supplied by slaves brought mainly from the west coast of Africa.

The slaves brought their native traditions of music and dance with them while the Spaniards brought the dances of Spain and Europe. Contradanzas and Waltzes were just two European dances that found their way into the dance salons of Cuba.

MUSICAL ACCOMPANIMENT The musical instruments of these countries also came to Cuba. From Spain came the guitar and castanets, while from Africa came the various drums, including bongos with the two differently toned drums, the maracas – roughly an egg-shaped sphere filled with dried beads on a handle – and the claves. The claves are two hard wood sticks that are beaten together to give a particular dominant clicking noise that is used to set and maintain the tempo. They are normally played in a syncopated two bar phrase and American band leaders taught their singers to use them by getting them to say, to themselves, 'shave, haircut, two bits'. Over a two bar phrase of 4/4 music the accents fall on the 1st, 4th, 7th quaver in the first bar and on the 3rd and 5th quaver in the second bar. While other syncopated rhythms are now used regularly this traditional two bar phrase is still almost always evident.

RHYTHMIC PATTERNS As might be expected in a dance where the music has such complex rhythmic patterns, the counting for the steps is not entirely straightforward. The forwards step of the basic

A group of dancers demonstrate the Rumba at the Nautilus Bath Club in Miami, Florida in 1932.

figures commences on the second crotchet in the bar of music. However, because the melody phrases in the tunes often start on the first crotchet, some beginners find the second beat rhythm a little difficult. At this stage, do not worry about this but concentrate on the foot patterns. In dance competitions the dancers will be dancing to the Cuban rhythm and their dance will be based on the figures described. Those who have had the

Carol Vorderman and Paul Killick perform the Rumba as their final dance in BBC TV's *Strictly Come Dancing*.

opportunity of seeing the brilliant Donnie Burns MBE and Gaynor Fairweather MBE, the Scottish winners of fourteen consecutive Professional World Latin Dance Championships, will have seen the dizzy heights the Rumba can achieve.

There are many similarities between Rumba, Cha Cha Cha and Salsa, and nearly all figures with slight amendments can be transferred from one rhythm to another in this trio of dances.

In the Rumba all steps are taken on the ball of the foot first and then the weight is allowed to settle over the foot, while the supporting leg straightens causing the hips to settle sideways. This action is explained in the Basic Movement and although it is not repeated in the other figures, it does take place throughout the dance.

THE HOLD For basic Rumba figures use an Open Hold (see page 18).

The Basic Movement

This figure is almost the same as the basic figure in Cha Cha Cha. The difference is the syncopations in the Cha Cha Cha. In this Basic Movement you should make a small turn to the left throughout, once you have mastered the steps. Over one full figure turn a quarter of a full turn, that is, if you start with your back to the nearest wall you should have your left shoulder facing the same wall at the end of one full basic figure.

		Man's Steps		**Lady's Steps**
Count:		**M**		**L**
Two	1	LEFT FOOT takes a small step forwards on the ball of the foot, taking weight onto flat foot at the end of the step and swinging hips to the left. Takes one beat of music.	1	RIGHT FOOT takes a small step backwards and, as weight transfers onto it, lift the heel of your left foot a little off the floor, swinging hips to the right. Takes one beat of music.
Three	2	RIGHT FOOT remains in place and weight transfers onto it, swinging hips to the right. Takes one beat of music.	2	LEFT FOOT remains in place, lowering heel as weight is taken forwards onto it and swinging hips to the left. Takes one beat of music.
Four-one	3	LEFT FOOT takes a step to the side on the ball of the foot and, as weight transfers onto foot, swinging hips to the left. Takes two beats of music.	3	RIGHT FOOT takes a step to the side on the ball of the foot and, as weight transfers onto foot, swinging hips to the right. Takes two beats of music.
Two	4	RIGHT FOOT takes a small step backwards and, as weight transfers onto it, lift the heel of your left foot a little off the floor, swinging hips to the right. Takes one beat of music.	4	LEFT FOOT takes a small step forwards on the ball of the foot, taking weight onto flat foot at the end of the step, swinging hips to the left. Takes one beat of music.
Three	5	LEFT FOOT remains in place, lowering heel as weight is taken forwards onto it and swinging hips to the left. Takes one beat of music.	5	RIGHT FOOT remains in place and weight transfers onto it, swinging hips to the right. Takes one beat of music.
Four-one	6	RIGHT FOOT takes a step to the side on ball of foot and, as weight transfers onto foot, swinging hips to the right. Takes two beats of music.	6	LEFT FOOT takes a step to the side on the ball of the foot and, as weight transfers onto foot, swinging hips to the left. Takes two beats of music.

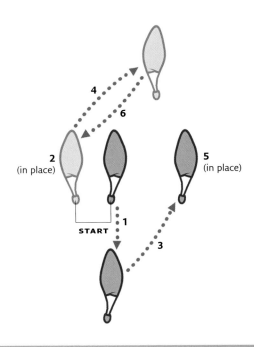

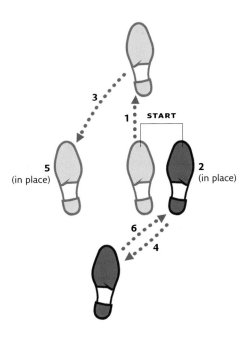

Side Cucarachas

Dance this figure after the Basic Movement and then follow it with the Basic Movement (see pages 210–1).

		Man's Steps			Lady's Steps
Count:		**M**			**L**
Two	1	LEFT FOOT takes a step to the side, pressing foot into floor so as to lever weight of body into next step.	1		RIGHT FOOT takes a step to the side, pressing foot into floor so as to lever weight of body into next step.
Three	2	RIGHT FOOT remains in place and full weight is taken onto it.	2		LEFT FOOT remains in place and full weight is taken onto it.
Four-one	3	LEFT FOOT closes to right foot.	3		RIGHT FOOT closes to left foot.
Two	4	RIGHT FOOT takes a step to the side, pressing foot into floor so as to lever weight of body into next step.	4		LEFT FOOT takes a step to the side, pressing foot into floor so as to lever weight of body into next step.
Three	5	LEFT FOOT remains in place and full weight is taken onto it.	5		RIGHT FOOT remains in place and full weight is taken onto it.
Four-one	6	RIGHT FOOT closes to left foot.	6		LEFT FOOT closes to right foot.

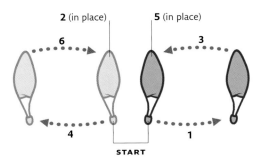

2 (in place) **5** (in place)

6

3

4

1

START

5 (in place) **2** (in place)

3

6

1

4

START

The Basic Movement

Two

Three

Four-one

1 **M** LEFT FOOT takes a step forwards, swinging hips to the left.
L RIGHT FOOT takes a step backwards, swinging hips to the right.
Takes one beat of music.

2 **M** RIGHT FOOT remains in place, weight back onto it, hips to the right.
L LEFT FOOT remains in place, weight forwards onto it, hips to the left.
Takes one beat of music.

3 **M** LEFT FOOT takes a step to the side, swinging hips to the left.
L RIGHT FOOT takes a step to the side, swinging hips to the right.
Takes two beats of music.

Side Cucarachas

Two

Three

Four-one

1 **M** LEFT FOOT to side, with pressure, so as to lever weight into next step.
L RIGHT FOOT to side, pressing into floor so as to lever weight into next step.

2 **M** RIGHT FOOT remains in place and full weight is taken onto it.
L LEFT FOOT remains in place and full weight is taken onto it.

3 **M** LEFT FOOT closes to right foot.
L RIGHT FOOT closes to left foot.

Two

4 **M** RIGHT FOOT takes a step backwards, swinging hips to the right.
L LEFT FOOT takes a step forwards, swinging hips to the left.
Takes one beat of music.

Three

5 **M** LEFT FOOT remains in place, weight forwards onto it, hips to the left.
L RIGHT FOOT remains in place, weight back onto it, hips to the right.
Takes one beat of music.

Four-one

6 **M** RIGHT FOOT takes a step to the side, swinging hips to the right.
L LEFT FOOT takes a step to the side, swinging hips to the left.
Takes two beats of music.

Two

4 **M** RIGHT FOOT to side, with pressure so as to lever weight into next step.
L LEFT FOOT to side, pressing into floor so as to lever weight into next step.

Three

5 **M** LEFT FOOT remains in place and full weight is taken onto it.
L RIGHT FOOT remains in place and full weight taken onto it.

Four-one

6 **M** RIGHT FOOT closes to left foot.
L LEFT FOOT closes to right foot.

The Opening Outs

This figure, danced in Open Hold (see page 18), is a variation on the Side Cucarachas (see pages 212–3). Like Cucarachas, the Opening Outs can also follow and be followed by the Basic Movement (see pages 210–1).

Man's Steps

Lady's Steps

Count:	**M**		**L**	
Two	**1**	LEFT FOOT takes a step to the side, pushing your partner with the left hand and then releasing hold, using pressure into the floor.	**1**	RIGHT FOOT takes a step backwards, turning about 90 degrees to the right and releasing hold of partner's hand from your right hand, using pressure into the floor.
Three	**2**	RIGHT FOOT remains in place and full weight is taken onto it, guiding the lady to step forwards.	**2**	LEFT FOOT remains in place and full weight is taken forwards onto it.
Four-one	**3**	LEFT FOOT closes to right foot, your partner turns to face you and you regain hold of her right hand with your left hand.	**3**	RIGHT FOOT takes a step to the side, turning to the left to face your partner and regain hold of his left hand with your right hand.
Two	**4**	RIGHT FOOT takes a step to the side, pushing your partner with the right hand and then releasing hold, using pressure into the floor.	**4**	LEFT FOOT takes a step backwards, turning about 90 degrees to the left and releasing hold of partner from left hand, using pressure into the floor.
Three	**5**	LEFT FOOT remains in place and full weight is taken onto it, guiding the lady to step forwards.	**5**	RIGHT FOOT remains in place and full weight is taken forwards onto it.
Four-one	**6**	RIGHT FOOT closes to left foot, partner turns to face you. Regain normal hold.	**6**	LEFT FOOT takes a step to the side, turning to the right to face your partner. Regain normal hold.

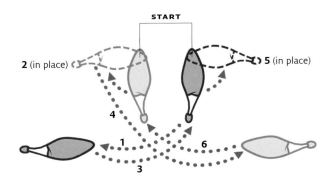

The New York

This figure can be followed by the Basic Movement (see pages 210–1) .

Man's Steps

Prior to dancing this figure check the left turn on step 6 of the Basic Movement and prepare to turn right.

Lady's Steps

In step 6 of the Basic Movement the man will have started to turn you a little to your left in preparation for the New York.

Count:		**M**		**L**
Two	1	LEFT FOOT steps forwards and across the right foot, releasing hold of your partner with your right hand. Lady steps forwards with you in open counter promenade position.	1	RIGHT FOOT steps forwards and across the left foot. The man will release hold of you with his right hand, bring your left hand up to shoulder level in open counter promenade position.
Three	2	RIGHT FOOT remains in place and weight is taken back onto it, starting to turn left.	2	LEFT FOOT remains in place and weight is taken back onto it, starting to turn right.
Four-one	3	LEFT FOOT takes a step to the side, turning to the left to face your partner, taking hold of her left hand in your right and releasing hold of her right hand from your left hand.	3	RIGHT FOOT takes a step to the side, turning to the right to face partner. Partner will release hold of your right hand from his left and at the same time take your left hand in his right.
Two	4	RIGHT FOOT forwards and across the left foot. The lady is stepping forwards with you in open promenade position.	4	LEFT FOOT takes a step forwards and across the right foot. The man is stepping forwards with you in open promenade position.
Three	5	LEFT FOOT remains in place and weight is taken back onto it, starting to turn to right.	5	RIGHT FOOT remains in place and weight is taken back onto it, starting to turn to left.
Four-one	6	RIGHT FOOT takes a step to the side, turning to the right to face your partner, regaining normal hold of her with her right hand in your left and your right hand on her back.	6	LEFT FOOT takes a step to the side, turning to the left to face partner, regaining normal hold of partner.

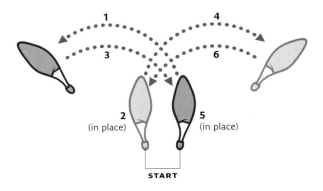

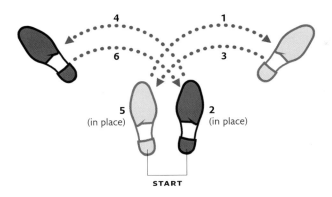

The Opening Outs

Two

Three

Four-one

1 **M** LEFT FOOT to side, guiding partner with left hand and then release hold.
  L RIGHT FOOT backwards, turning about 90 degrees to the right.

2 **M** RIGHT FOOT remains in place, weight is taken onto it, leading lady to step forwards.
  L LEFT FOOT remains in place and take full weight onto it.

3 **M** LEFT FOOT closes to right foot, regaining hold of partner's right hand.
  L RIGHT FOOT to side, turning to left to face partner and regain hold of his hand.

The New York

Two

Three

Four-one

1 **M** LEFT FOOT forwards and across right foot, releasing hold with right hand.
  L RIGHT FOOT forwards and across left foot in open counter promenade position.

2 **M** RIGHT FOOT remains in place, weight back onto it, starting to turn left.
  L LEFT FOOT remains in place, weight back onto it, starting to turn right.

3 **M** LEFT FOOT to side, turn to face partner, take hold of her left hand, let go of her right hand.
  L RIGHT FOOT to side, turning to right to face partner.

Two

4 M RIGHT FOOT to side, guiding partner with right hand and then release hold.
L LEFT FOOT backwards, turning about 90 degrees to the left.

Three

5 M LEFT FOOT remains in place and weight is taken onto it, guiding the lady to step forwards.
L RIGHT FOOT remains in place, full weight is taken onto it.

Four-one

6 M RIGHT FOOT closes to left foot, turning partner to face you and regain normal hold.
L LEFT FOOT to side turning to right to face partner.

Two

4 M RIGHT FOOT forwards and across left foot, in open promenade position.
L LEFT FOOT forwards and across right foot in open promenade position.

Three

5 M LEFT FOOT remains in place, weight back onto it, starting to turn right.
L RIGHT FOOT remains in place and weight back onto it, starting to turn left.

Four-one

6 M RIGHT FOOT to side, turning to face partner, regaining normal hold.
L LEFT FOOT to side, turning to left to face partner, regaining normal hold.

Carole Lombard and George Raft dancing in the 1935 film, *Rumba*.

The Fan

In this figure of three steps (steps 4–6), the man turns the lady so that her body is at right angles to his. However, here, the first three steps (steps 1–3) of the Basic Movement (see page 210–1) are included. Follow this with the Hockey Stick (see pages 226–7).

	Man's Steps		Lady's Steps

Count:	**M**		**L**
Two 1	LEFT FOOT takes a small step forwards.	1	RIGHT FOOT takes a small step backwards.
Three 2	RIGHT FOOT remains in place and the weight is taken back onto it.	2	LEFT FOOT remains in place and the weight is taken forwards onto it.
Four-one 3	LEFT FOOT takes a step to the side, turning slightly to the left and lowering your left hand.	3	RIGHT FOOT takes a step to the side, turning slightly to the right and lowering your right hand.
Two 4	RIGHT FOOT takes a step backwards, leading the lady to step across and in front of you.	4	LEFT FOOT takes a step forwards across in front of the man.
Three 5	LEFT FOOT remains in place and the weight is taken forwards onto it, turning the lady to her left by pulling your left hand back and pushing her with your right hand and then releasing hold of her with that hand.	5	RIGHT FOOT takes a step forwards, turning to the left on the ball of your foot, to finish with right foot back. The man will guide you into the turn and then release hold of you from his right hand.
Four-one 6	RIGHT FOOT takes a small step to the side, turning a little to the left to finish at right angles to your partner and almost at arm's length.	6	LEFT FOOT takes a step backwards, still turning to finish at right angles to your partner and almost at arm's length.

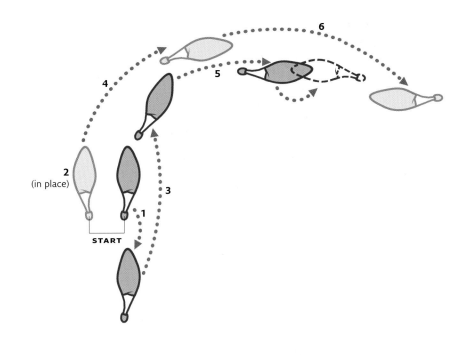

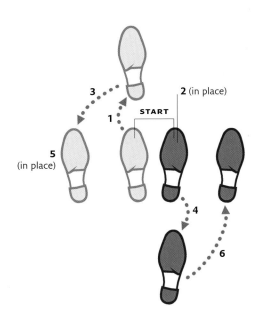

The Hockey Stick

Precede the Hockey Stick with the Fan (see pages 224–5). At the end of this figure you are left slightly apart from your partner with the man holding the lady's right hand in his left hand. To regain normal hold, dance the first half of the Basic Movement (see pages 210–1); the man should pull the lady gently towards him.

Man's Steps

Lady's Steps

Count:		**M**		**L**
Two	1	LEFT FOOT takes a step forwards, keeping left hand relaxed so that lady can close her right foot to left foot.	1	RIGHT FOOT closes to left foot, remaining slightly away from the man on this step.
Three	2	RIGHT FOOT remains in place and the weight is taken back onto it, leading the lady to start moving forwards with your left hand.	2	LEFT FOOT takes a step forwards, starting to move across and in front of the man.
Four-one	3	LEFT FOOT closes to right foot, still leading the lady forwards (the 90 degree angle between you at end of the Fan means the lady will move in front of you). Raise your left and the lady's right hand to form an arch.	3	RIGHT FOOT takes a step forwards across the front of the man. The man raises your right hand so that you both form an arch for you to turn under.
Two	4	RIGHT FOOT takes a step backwards, turning slightly to the right and turning the lady to her left with an anti-clockwise movement of your left hand. Do not grip her hand tightly, allowing it to turn in yours.	4	LEFT FOOT takes a step forwards, starting to turn left under the arch formed by your right and the man's left arms.
Three	5	LEFT FOOT remains in place and the weight is taken forwards onto it, still turning the lady and allowing your hand to lower down to just above waist level.	5	RIGHT FOOT takes a step forwards, turning left on the ball of your foot to face partner, to finish with right foot back and his left hand holding your right at waist level.
Four-one	6	RIGHT FOOT steps forwards towards partner with left hand lowered.	6	LEFT FOOT takes a small step backwards.

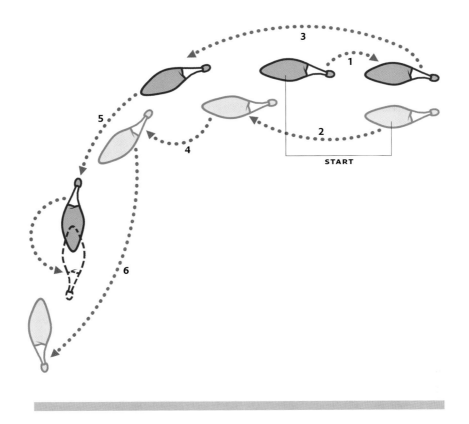

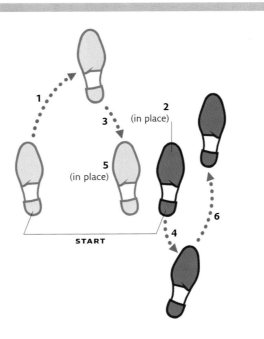

The Fan

Two	*Three*	*Four-one*

1   **M** LEFT FOOT takes a step forwards.
    L RIGHT FOOT takes a step backwards.

2   **M** RIGHT FOOT remains in place and weight is taken back onto it.
    L LEFT FOOT remains in place and weight is taken forwards onto it.

3   **M** LEFT FOOT steps to side, turning slightly to left and lowering left hand.
    L RIGHT FOOT steps to side, turning slightly to right and lowering right hand.

The Hockey Stick

Two	*Three*	*Four-one*

1   **M** LEFT FOOT takes a step forwards, keeping left hand relaxed.
    L RIGHT FOOT closes to left foot.

2   **M** RIGHT FOOT remains in place, weight taken back onto it, leading lady to start moving forwards.
    L LEFT FOOT takes a step forwards, starting to move in front of man.

3   **M** LEFT FOOT closes to right foot, still leading lady forwards, raising left hand to form an arch.
    L RIGHT FOOT forwards in front of man.

Top row

Two

Three

Four-one

4 **M** RIGHT FOOT takes a step backwards, leading lady to step across and in front of you.
  L LEFT FOOT takes a step forwards in front of man.

5 **M** LEFT FOOT remains in place, weight is taken onto it, turn lady to her left and release hold.
  L RIGHT FOOT takes a step forwards, turning left to end with right foot back.

6 **M** RIGHT FOOT steps to side turning a little to left.
  L LEFT FOOT backwards, still turning to finish at right angles to the man and almost at arm's length.

Bottom row

Two

Three

Four-one

4 **M** RIGHT FOOT backwards, turning slightly to the right and turning lady to her left.
  L LEFT FOOT takes a step forwards, start turning left under the arch.

5 **M** LEFT FOOT remains in place, weight is taken forwards onto it, still turning lady.
  L RIGHT FOOT forwards, turning left to end with right foot back.

6 **M** RIGHT FOOT takes a step forwards towards partner, lowering left hand.
  L LEFT FOOT takes a small step backwards.

Natural Top

In this figure the man and lady circle around a central point as though they were moving around the rim of and at opposite sides of a wheel. Commence after step 3 of the Basic Movement (see pages 210–1), but make the turn slightly to the right. The close hold (see page 18) is retained throughout and the Natural Top can be followed by steps 4–6 of the Basic Movement.

Once you have mastered the foot pattern, you can increase the amount of turn as shown in the step-by-step photographs.

Count:		Man's Steps			Lady's Steps
		M			**L**
Two	1	RIGHT FOOT crosses behind left foot placing right toe near to left heel, turning strongly to the right.	1		LEFT FOOT takes a step to the side and slightly backwards, starting to turn strongly to the right.
Three	2	LEFT FOOT steps to the side and slightly forwards, still turning to the right.	2		RIGHT FOOT forwards and across left foot, still turning to the right.
Four-one	3	RIGHT FOOT crosses behind left foot, placing right toe near to left heel, turning strongly to the right.	3		LEFT FOOT steps to the side and slightly backwards, still turning to the right.
Two	4	LEFT FOOT steps to the side and slightly forwards, still turning to the right.	4		RIGHT FOOT forwards and across left foot, still turning to the right.
Three	5	RIGHT FOOT crosses behind left foot, placing right toe near to left heel, turning strongly to the right.	5		LEFT FOOT steps to the side and slightly backwards, still turning to the right.
Four-one	6	LEFT FOOT steps to the side and slightly forwards, completing the turn to the right.	6		RIGHT FOOT forwards and across left foot, completing the turn to the right.

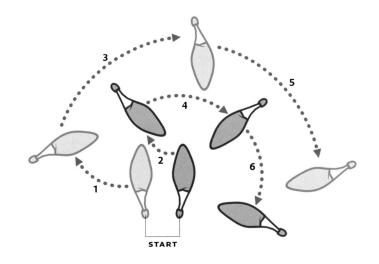

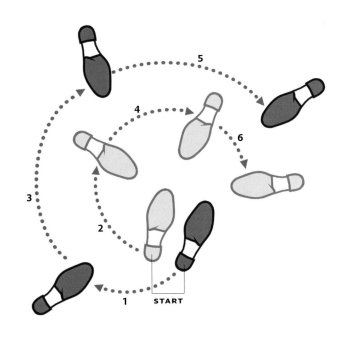

Throughout all the Rumba figures, steps are taken on the ball of the foot first and then the weight settles over the foot, while the supporting leg straightens causing the hips to settle sideways.

Natural Top

Two

Three

Four-one

1 **M** RIGHT FOOT crosses behind left foot placing right toe near to left heel, turning strongly to right.
L LEFT FOOT to side and backwards, starting to turn strongly to right.

2 **M** LEFT FOOT to side and slightly forwards, still turning to right.
L RIGHT FOOT forwards and across left foot, still turning to right.

3 **M** RIGHT FOOT crosses behind left foot placing right toe near to left heel, turning strongly to right.
L LEFT FOOT side and slightly backwards, still turning to right.

Two

Three

Four-one

4 **M** LEFT FOOT to side and slightly forwards, still turning to right.
L RIGHT FOOT forwards and across left foot ,still turning to right.

5 **M** RIGHT FOOT crosses behind left foot placing right toe near to left heel, turning strongly to right.
L LEFT FOOT to side and slightly backwards, still turning to right.

6 **M** LEFT FOOT to side, completing the turn to the right.
L RIGHT FOOT forwards and across left foot, completing the turn to the right.

Disco / Freestyle

John Travolta epitomizes the Disco trend of the 1970s in the film *Saturday Night Fever* (1977).

To the uninitiated, Disco dancing can often look like completely wild and undisciplined movements of the limbs, but to aficionados this dance form is capable of analysis. You can learn the dance in a way that will give the fullest enjoyment of the expression of the music.

Among the current popular dances, Disco, also called Freestyle, is different from most in that it is danced solo. Also, it is not danced to a set sequence, as is the case in line dancing, for example. With the exception of specialist clubs that feature Salsa, Argentine Tango, and so on, Disco is the dance of the club culture. However, the music is all pervasive and everyone can enjoy the dance irrespective of age.

MOVEMENT As might be expected, it is necessary to approach the dance in a rather different way from that employed for the traditional forms of ballroom dancing. Each part of the body is involved. Movements can be made in four fundamental ways: turning or rotating, tilting, lifting, and bending. These actions can apply to almost any part of the body – head, arms, legs and body torso. This is best illustrated with a few examples.

Turning your head to look left or right are examples of 'turning'. Keeping the eyeline straight in front and then tilting the head to look up and dropping the chin down onto the chest are 'tilting'. Raising your shoulders as in shrugging is 'lifting'.

Studio 54 in New York – the fashionable Disco club everyone was keen to visit in the early 1980s.

Bending the arm at the elbow is 'bending'. All these actions fit to the strong beat of the music and usually take place concurrently on the same beat of music. The following basic units will get you started and you are in the happy position of not needing a partner and only needing the minimum of space.

THE 'STEPS' Unlike other dances there are no universally agreed 'movements' in Disco. In this section there are a few basic routines to get you started, and they have been given names purely as an aid to memory. Again, unlike other dances, the steps are the same for the man and the lady. In all descriptions each 'step' takes one beat of music. Try the basics that follow to slow music first, until you are sure that you can dance them, and then gradually increase the music speed. Because this is an entirely non-progressive dance you can face in any direction for the various figures.

Liza Minnelli and Mikhail Baryshnikov dancing at the hedonistic Studio 54 in New York in 1977.

Head Turns

Start with the feet a few inches apart, with the weight over your right foot, looking forwards with both hands held loosely at sides of the body. The eight steps that follow take eight beats of music (two bars) in common or 4/4 time and use legs and head only.

Four

4 REPEAT step 2 but take the weight onto the left foot.

One

5 RIGHT FOOT takes a small step to the side without weight, with toe pointed. Keep the weight on left foot and turn your head to the right, with arms at your side.

Two

6 RIGHT FOOT closes back to the starting position near to left foot. Keep the weight on left foot and turn your head forwards, with arms still at your side.

Head Turns

One

1 LEFT FOOT takes a small step to the side without weight, with toe pointed to the floor and heel slightly raised. Keep the weight on right foot and turn head left, with arms at your side.

Two

2 LEFT FOOT closes back to the starting position near to right foot. Keep the weight on right foot and turn head forwards, with arms still at your side.

Three

3 REPEAT step 1.

Three

7 REPEAT step 5.

Four

8 REPEAT STEP 6 but take the weight onto the right foot.

Head Turns and Hand Movement

You will see that this is merely the Head Turns figure (see page 238–9) with the addition of simple hand actions that will help your co-ordination. Start with the weight on your right foot. Each movement or step takes one beat of music.

Four

4 REPEAT step 2 but take the weight onto the left foot.

One

5 RIGHT FOOT takes a small step to the side, with toe pointed towards the floor. Keep the weight on left foot and turn your head to the right, raising your right hand upwards.

Two

6 RIGHT FOOT closes back to the starting position. Keep the weight on the left foot and turn your head to look forwards again, with arms at the side of your body.

Head Turns and Hand Movement

One

1 LEFT FOOT takes a small step to the side. Keep the weight on the right foot with toe pointed to the floor and turn head to the left, raising left hand upwards.

Two

2 LEFT FOOT closes back to the starting position. Keep the weight on the right foot and turn your head to look forwards again, with arms at the side of your body.

Three

3 REPEAT step 1.

Three

7 REPEAT step 5.

Four

8 REPEAT step 6 but take the weight onto the right foot.

Springy Knees

The bending of the knee should take place on the heaviest beats in the bar of music and you should experiment until you feel what you are doing fits the music best. As an alternative, you can pause on the first beat of music, then bend your knees on the second beat. Start with the weight on both your feet.

Springy Knees

One

1 BEND both knees.

Two

2 STRAIGHTEN knees.

Hip Rolls

Those of you who have used a hoola hoop should find this very straightforward because a hip roll requires the same movement. The action can be repeated. It is described as rotating right first but, of course, you can rotate left first. Raw beginners can take one beat of music for each of the counts but, as soon as possible, try to speed this up, until eventually you can complete one full rotation in two beats of music. Start with the weight on both your feet.

Hip Rolls

One

1 PUSH YOUR HIPS forwards with your knees bent and weight over both feet.

Three

3 BEND both knees.

Four

4 STRAIGHTEN knees.

Two

2 ROTATE THE HIPS to the right side with a circular movement.

Three

3 PULL THE HIPS backwards.

Four

4 ROTATE THE HIPS to the left side, with a circular movement.

Head, Hands, Feet and Knees

This group of steps brings together several of the basic actions detailed in the other Disco movements. Start with the weight on the right foot with knees slightly bent. Each movement or step takes one beat of music.

Head, Hands, Feet and Knees

One

1 LEFT FOOT takes a small step forwards and to the side, keeping weight on right foot. Push left hip upwards and forwards, turn head left and raise left hand upwards.

Two

2 LEFT FOOT closes to right foot, still keeping weight on right foot and bringing hips back to normal position. Turn your head forwards and lower your hand and arm to your side.

Two

6 RIGHT FOOT closes to left foot, still keeping weight on left foot and bringing the hips back to normal position. Turn your head forwards and lower your hand and arm to your side.

Three

7 REPEAT step 5.

Four

8 RIGHT FOOT closes to left foot, taking weight back onto it, and bringing the hips back to the normal position. Turn your head forwards and lower your hand and arm to your side.

Three

3 REPEAT step 1.

Four

4 LEFT FOOT closes to right foot taking the weight back onto it and bringing the hips back to normal position. Turn your head forwards and lower your hand and arm to your side.

One

5 RIGHT FOOT takes a small step forwards and to the side, keeping weight on left foot. Push right hip upwards and forwards, turn head right and raise right hand upwards.

Shoulder Shimmy or Boob Trembler

When you are really comfortable with the figure, the more lissom of you can add the Hip Rolls (see pages 242–3) or hoola hoop type movements .

Start with the weight equally placed over both feet and knees slightly bent. Hold the hands forwards so that the forearms are roughly parallel to the floor but also relaxed.

Shoulder Shimmy or Boob Trembler

One

1 RIGHT SHOULDER forwards and left shoulder backwards. Takes one beat of music.

Two

2 LEFT SHOULDER forwards and right shoulder backwards. Takes one beat of music.

Faster Shoulder Shimmy or Boob Trembler

Left shoulder forwards then right shoulder forwards on the count of 'one' and repeat for each count. This is double the speed of the Shoulder Shimmy on page 245, but even this is not fast enough.

Try to double the speed again until you can fit the 'left, right, left, right' combination to each beat of music.

Faster Shoulder Shimmy or Boob Trembler

One

Two

1 LEFT SHOULDER forwards.

2 RIGHT SHOULDER forwards.

The Twist

One

Two

1 TAKE WEIGHT FORWARDS onto balls of feet without raising the heels from floor. Move balls of feet so that heels shift to left and toes point to right, move your hands leftwards.

2 WITH WEIGHT on the balls of the feet, turn so that the heels move to the right and the toes point to left, at the same time move your hands rightwards.

The Twist

Solo dancing became popular in the 1960s when Chubby Checker released the pop records, 'Let's Twist' and 'Let's Twist Again'. It is a while ago now but the basic movement is still seen on the dancing scene and it is well within the reach of inexperienced dancers.

Start with the feet a few inches apart, with the weight on both feet and with your knees slightly bent. Hold your hands at about waist level, a little in front of the body. It might help to imagine that you are holding something, say a small book, between them or even holding one hand in the other.

Repeat steps 1 and 2 as many times as you fancy.

Often dancers add a little spice to the action by bending the knees more and more as the action continues. It is possible to carry on until you are nearly kneeling on the floor (see 4 below).

Three

3 REPEAT STEP 1 then step 2. Repeat these steps as often as you wish.

Variation

4 ADD SPICE to the action – continue twisting until your knees are fully bent and you are close to the floor. Your arms should help you to balance.

Twist again

5 GRADUALLY TWIST yourself up to the starting position, ready to 'twist again'.

Glossary

4/4 Time: A musical term, sometimes called common time, to indicate that there are four crotchets, or beats, in each bar of music, as in the Foxtrot.

3/4 Time: A similar musical term indicating three crotchets or beats in each bar of music, as in the Waltz.

Backing diagonally to centre: An indication of where the dancer is in relation to the movement of the dance around the room. Stand with the nearest wall on your left side and your body at right angles to it – to be 'backing diagonally to centre', turn 45 degrees to the left.

Backing diagonally to wall: An indication of where the dancer is in relation to the movement of the dance around the room. The 'wall' in the term is the one along which the dance will progress. Stand with the nearest wall on your left side and your body at right angles to it – to be 'backing diagonally to wall' turn 45 degrees to the right.

Backing line of dance: When the dancer is backing the imaginary line of dance (see Line of dance) then he or she is 'backing line of dance'.

Body sway: From a vertical position a tilt of the body to the left or the right is known as 'body sway' and will be used naturally to lean slightly in towards the centre of rotation of turning dance figures.

Body swing: This refers to the momentum the body achieves when dancing freely and which helps create a smooth flowing dance.

Dance patterns: The various steps and figures used in dancing make patterns on the floor that are called 'dance patterns'.

Facing diagonally to centre: An indication of where the dancer is in relation to the movement of the dance round the room. Stand with the nearest wall on your right side and your body at right angles to it,

then turn 45 degrees to the left to be 'facing diagonally to centre'.

Facing diagonally to wall: An indication of where the dancer is in relation to the movement of the dance round the room. Face the line of dance (see below), then turn 45 degrees to the right to be 'facing diagonally to wall'.

Facing line of dance: Face the imaginary line defined as the line of dance (see below).

Fall-away position: For ballroom and Latin dances, stand in the promenade position, then the man's left foot takes a step backwards and the lady's right foot takes a step backwards.

Fast syncopation: Syncopation is variance of the basic rhythm either by changing the emphasis or interloping additional beats or omitting beats. 'Fast syncopation' in dance is when a string of rapidly interpolated steps are inserted into the basic rhythmic pattern.

Figure: A series of steps linked together as one unit.

Foot marks time in place: The foot remains in place but the weight of your body is transferred onto it.

Foot remains in place: The foot remains in the position previously achieved and the weight of your body is retained on it.

Hip action: Movement of the hips from the waist down. Mostly laterally from left to right but can be forwards and backwards.

Leg swing: The free movement of the leg with the hip as fulcrum, from one position to another.

Line of dance: The line of dance is an imaginary line parallel with the wall along which the dance moves. It progresses in an anti-clockwise direction around the room, and in a rectangular room it turns 90 degrees at each corner.

Normal position: In each dance the man and the lady mostly hold one another in a manner peculiar to that dance. The hold for the majority of the dance is referred to

as the 'normal position'. Variants will occur from time to time and will be defined as required.

Open counter promenade position (Latin): Face your partner, then turn 45 degrees, the man to the right and the lady to the left. The man holds the lady's right hand in his left hand and the free arms are held to the side.

Open promenade position (Latin): Face your partner, then turn 45 degrees, the man to the left and the lady to the right. The man holds the lady's left hand in his right hand and the free arms are held to the side.

Outside partner: A forwards step usually on the right foot to your left of both your partner's feet. It may also be left foot forwards to your right of both your partner's feet.

Partner outside: A backwards step on either foot where your partner is stepping forwards 'outside partner' (see above).

Polka rhythms: Steps taken with a slight jumping action from ball of foot to ball of foot.

Promenade position: From the close hold (ballroom), the man turns his body to the left away from the lady. The Lady turns her right side away from the man to form a V-shape. From the open hold (Latin), both the man and the lady turn outwards from each other – the man to the left and the lady to the right, forming a V shape.

Rhythm break, rightwards or leftwards: A sideways group of steps using the basic rhythm of the dance but not closing feet neatly.

Skipping steps: Steps taken with a slight forwards jump of supporting foot as other foot moves to its next position.

Directory

Choosing a dance studio

How do you select an appropriate school? Your main concern should be to ensure that your teacher has one of the three major qualification levels in one of the recognized teachers' organizations.

Under the heading 'Teachers' Organizations' you will see listed eight different bodies. The membership of each of these consists of dance teachers who have passed the appropriate examinations of the organization. They are all members of, and are overseen by, a loosely knit body known as the British Dance Council, and all conform to common standards. If you contact them they will let you know their members in your area.

There are three levels of qualification. In ascending order they are: Associate (A), Licentiate (L) – sometimes called Member (M) – and Fellow (F), the highest level. The name of the association or society is often abbreviated to initials.

In respect of the dances included in this book teachers can have qualified by examination in either a ballroom branch (BB) or a Latin branch (LA) of the appropriate body and this will sometimes be added to the qualification. For example, Lyndon Wainwright FIDTA (BB & LA) and Lynda King FIDTA (BB & LA) – Fellow of the International Dance Teachers' Association (Ballroom and Latin Branches).

Finally, many people are put off joining a school of dance by feelings of inadequacy or embarrassment. It is a great mistake. Dance teachers do realize this and you will be made welcome and made to feel comfortable irrespective of your previous experience.

UK DANCE ORGANIZATIONS

Ballroom Dancers' Federation
12 Warren Lodge Drive
Kingswood
SURREY KT20 6QN
Fax: 01737 833737

Ballroom Dancers' Federation International
PO Box 2075 Kenley
SURREY CR8 5YP
Fax: 020 87631368

British Dance Council
Terpsichore House
240 Merton Road
South Wimbledon
LONDON SW19 1EQ
Tel: 020 8545 0085
Fax: 020 8545 0225

Central Council of Physical Recreation
Francis House, Francis Street
LONDON SW1P 1DE
Tel: 020 7854 8500
Fax: 020 7854 8501
www.ccpr.org.uk

Council for Dance Education and Training
Toynbee Hall
28 Commercial Street
LONDON E1 6LS
Tel: 020 7247 4030
Fax: 020 7247 3404
www.cdet.org.uk

Germany

World Dance and Dance Sport Council
Karolinastrassa 20
28195 BREMEN
Tel: +49 421 13162
Fax: +49 421 14942

TEACHERS' ORGANIZATIONS

Allied Dancing Association
137 Greenhill Road
LIVEROOL L18 7HQ
Tel: 0151 724 1829

British Association of Teachers of Dancing
23 Marywood Square
GLASGOW G41 2BP
Scotland
Tel: 0141 423 4029
www.batd.co.uk

Imperial Society of Teachers of Dancing
22–26 Paul Street
LONDON EC2A 4QE
Tel: 020 7377 1577
Fax: 020 7247 8979
www.istd.org

International Dance Teachers' Association
76 Bennett Road
BRIGHTON BN2 5JL
Tel: 01273 685652
Fax: 01273 674388
www.idta.co.uk

National Association of Teachers of Dancing
44–47 The Broadway
THATCHAM
Berkshire RG19 3HP
Tel: 01635 868888
Fax: 01635 872301
www.natd.org.uk

Northern Counties Dance Teachers' Association
67 Elizabeth Drive
Palmersville
NEWCASTLE-UPON-TYNE
Tyne & Wear NE12 9QP
Tel: 0191 268 1830

Scottish Dance Teachers' Alliance
101 Park Road
GLASGOW G4 9JE
Tel: 0141 339 8944
Fax: 0141 357 4994

United Kingdom Alliance
Centenary House
38–40 Station Road
BLACKPOOL
Lancs FY4 1EU
Tel: 01253 408828
Fax: 01253 408066

DANCE STUDIOS

England

Bedfordshire
Dance Fantasia
15 The Magpies
Bushmead
LUTON LU2 7XT
Tel: 01582-488529
Rayners School of Dancing
The Hall
Ashwell Avenue
Sundon Park
LUTON LU3 3AU
Tel: 01582 592510

Berkshire
Ken and Blanche Bateman Studio of Ballroom Dancing
23 Buckingham Avenue East
SLOUGH SL1 3EB
Tel/Fax 01753 520003
Spotlights Dance Centre
15 Marks Road
WOKINGHAM RG41 1NR
Tel: 0118 979 5044
www.spotlightsdance.com

Buckinghamshire
The Jill Foster Dance Centre
130 Wolverton Road
Stony Stratford
MILTON KEYNES MK11 1DN
Tel: 01908 563029
The Suzanne Lear School of Dancing
24 Sospel Court
FARNHAM ROYAL SL2 3BT
Tel: 01753 644612
Tracey's Dancezone
14 Cressey Avenue
Shenley Brook End
MILTON KEYNES MK5 7EL
Tel: 01908 504271

Cambridgeshire
Brown's Dance Studio
286 Lincoln Road
PETERBOROUGH PE3 9PJ
Tel: 01733 554282
DMJ Dancing
8 Othello Close
Hartford
HUNTINGDON PE29 1SU
Tel: 01480 458522/07803 184826
Maureen's School of Dancing
14 Augustus Way
CHATTERIS PE16 6DR
Tel: 01354 693218

Cheshire

Dance Fever
2 Ashfield House
Ashfield Road
SALE M33 7FE
Tel: 07973 921714
www.dancefever.uk.com

Lucy Diamond School of Dancing
Middlewich British Legion and
Centura Club
MIDDLEWICH
Tel: 07929 051917

J. J. Foulds School of Dancing
Ashpoole House
LOWTON WA3 1BG
Tel: 01942 671270

Northwich Dance Company
c/o 16 Mayfair Drive
Kingsmead
NORTHWICH CW9 8GF
Tel: 01606 49050

Village Dancentre
9 Park Road Hale
ALTRINCHAM WA15 9NL
(Classes in Bowdon, Hazel
Grove and Offerton)
Tel: 0161 928 9705

Cornwall

Tyler School of Dancing
'Topspin'
32 Trenance Avenue
NEWQUAY TR7 2HQ
Tel: 01637 873789

Derbyshire

Samantha-Jane Loades Academy of Dance
36a Frederick Avenue
ILKESTON DE7 4DW
Tel: 0115 932 3560/07946
389497

Devon

Chance to Dance
65 Churchill Road
EXMOUTH EX8 4DT
Tel: 01395 269782

Dance Latino
Renmark House 26 Elm Road
EXMOUTH EX8 2LG
Tel: 01395 277217

Lansdowne Dance Centre
16 Cadeell Park Road
TORQUAY TQ2 7JU
Tel: 01803 613580

Tanner-J Dance Zone
12 Redvers Grove

Plympton
PLYMOUTH PL7 1HU
Tel: 01752 283828

Westcountry Dance Studios
Inglenook Rockbeare Hill
EXETER EX5 2EZ
Tel: 01404 822942

Dorset

Bridport School of Dancing and Lyric Studios Stagecraft
9 Barrack Street
BRIDPORT DT6 3L4
Tel: 01308 427769

Dance Majic
Newtown Liberal Hall
316 Ringwood Road
Parkstone
POOLE
Tel: 01202 723381
www.dorsetdancecentre.co.uk

Durham

Lee Green Dance Centre
5 Lee Green
NEWTON AYCLIFFE DL5 5HN
Tel: 01325 318239

Richardson's Dance Studio
27-28 Fore Bondgate
BISHOP AUCKLAND DL14 7PE
Tel: 01388 609899
www.richardsonsdance
studio.co.uk

Essex

Anderson Dance Group
226 Perry Street
BILLERICAY CM12 0NZ
Tel: 01277 633509
www.andersondancegroup.
co.uk

A and M Dancing
5 St Mary's Road
BRAINTREE CM7 3JP
Tel: 01376 325753

Athene School of Dancing
Church Green
Broomfield
CHELMSFORD CM1 7BD
Tel: 0845 004 3062
www.pleisuredance.biz

King's Palais of Dance
WCA Market Road
WICKFORD SS12 0AG
Tel: 01375 375810

Spotlight DanceWorld
739A London Road
WESTCLIFF-ON-SEA SS0 9ST
Tel: 01702 474374

Steps Ahead School of Dancing
10 Griffith Close

Chadwell Heath
ROMFORD RM8 1TW
Tel: 07739 314596
www.stepsaheaddancing.com

Western Dance Centre
38 High Street
HADLEIGH SS9 2PB
Tel: 01702 559836
www.westerndancecentre.co.uk

Gloucestershire

Dancestars
37 Parry Road
GLOUCESTER GL1 4RZ
Tel: 01452 423 234

Foot Tappers School of Dancing
55 Dunster Close
TUFFLEY GL4 0TP
Tel: 01452 419324

Greater London

CK's Academy of Dance
Correspondence: 16 St Marks
Road
Bush Hill Park
ENFIELD EN1 1BE
Tel: 020 8482 4885
www.ckdance.co.uk

Dance Dayz
171 Henley Avenue
North Cheam
SUTTON SM3 9SD
Tel: 020 8641 5492

Dance Unlimited
74 Beresford Avenue
SURBITON KT5 9LW
Tel: 020 8339 8875
www.dance-unlimited.org

Hotsteps Dance Club
11B Station Road
ORPINGTON BR6 0RZ
Tel: 01689 822702
www.hotsteps.co.uk

Langley School of Dancing
Shepperton Village Hall
High Street
SHEPPERTON TW17 9AU
Tel: 020 8751 2177
www.langleydancing.co.uk

Pam's Dance Vogue
73 Hoylake Crescent
ICKENHAM UB10 8JQ
Tel: 01895 632143

Charles Richman
31 St Andrews Avenue
HORNCHURCH RM12 5DU
Tel: 07956 957038

Rita Sinclair
c/o 117 Burnway
HORNCHURCH RM11 3SW

Tel: 01708 471208/07887
511468

Wedding and Emergency Dance Lessons
The Dance Matrix – Nationwide
Head Office: 115 Crofton Way
ENFIELD EN2 8HR
www.dancematrix.com

Wright Rhythm Dancing School
133 First Avenue
Bush Hill Park
ENFIELD EN1 1BP
Tel: 07801 414959

Yvonne's Dance School
12 Matlock Crescent
CHEAM SM3 9SP
www.dance-technique.co.uk

Hampshire

Angela's School of Dancing
Queens Road
ALDERSHOT GU11 3JE
Tel: 01252 332239

Basingstoke Dance Centre
25 Cavalier Road
Old Basing
BASINGSTOKE RG24 0EW
Tel: 01256 461665

Dance Connection of Gosport
Brune Park Community School
Military Road
GOSPORT PO12 3BJ
Tel: 01329 314061/
023 8046 6181
www.groups.msn.co.uk/dance
connectionofgosport

Diamond Dancentre
9 Queens Road
FARNBOROUGH GU14 6DJ
Tel: 01252 342118
www.diamonddancentre.
co.uk

Diment Macdonald Dance Centre
10 Spring Crescent
Portswood
SOUTHAMPTON SO17 2GA
Tel: 023 8055 4192
www.dimentmacdonald.co.uk

Fiesta Dance School
Trimdon
Poland
ODIHAM RG29 1JL
Tel: 01256 395110

Footsteps Dance School
73 Britten Road
Brighton Hill
BASINGSTOKE RG22 4HN
Tel: 01256 475619

Shuffles Dance Studio
Oak Farm Community
School
Chaucer Road
FARNBOROUGH
Tel: 01252 314291/07774
151545
www.shuffles-dance.com
Spinners Dance Studio
4 Pardoe Close
Hedge End
SOUTHAMPTON SO30 0NE
Tel 01489 781513

Herefordshire
**Allseasons School of
Dance and Leisure**
35 Friar Street
HEREFORD HR4 0AS
Tel:01432 353756
www.allseasonsdance.co.uk
**Maureen's School of
Dancing**
41 Greengage Rise
Melbourn
ROYSTON SG8 6DS.
Tel: 01763 261680

Hertfordshire
Apton Dance Studio
Part Millers Two
The Maltings
BISHOPS STORTFORD
CM23 3DH
Tel: 01279 465381
www.aptondancestudio.com
The Dance Centre
1st Floor
24–26 High Street
HEMEL HEMPSTEAD HP1 3AE
Tel: 01442 252367

Kent
J. B.'s Dance Studio
90 St Michaels Street
FOLKESTONE CT20 1LS
Tel: 01303 252706
**Hurcombe School of
Dancing**
34 Oxen Lease
Singleton
ASHFORD TN23 4YT
Tel: 01233 643411
**Nicola Hyland School of
Dancing**
Sturry Social Centre
Sturry
NR. CANTERBURY
Tel: 07710 566827
**Page/Mason School of
Dancing**
7 St Peter's Court

BROADSTAIRS CT10 2UU
Tel: 01843 863730
Rose School of Dancing
8 Bearsted Close
GILLINGHAM ME8 6LS
Tel: 01634 360105/235878

Lancashire
Haslingden Dance Centre
IDL Club George Street
Haslingden
ROSSENDALE
Tel: 01706 228693
Liberal School of Dancing
114 Burnley Road
Broadclough
BACUP OL13 8DB
Tel: 01706 872556
**Northern Dance
Connection**
12 Holly Close
Clayton Le Woods
CHORLEY PR6 7JN
Tel: 01772 314551
www.dancefreeman.com

Leicestershire
118 Dance Studio
118 Charles Street
LEICESTER LE1 1LB
Tel: 0116 251 7073/289 2518
Premier Dancing Ltd
29–31 New Bond Street
LEICESTER LE1 4RQ
Tel: 0116 269 3618/251 1084
www.premierdance.co.uk

Lincolnshire
Cliftons Dance Academy
3 Turnberry Approach
Waltham
GRIMSBY DN37 0UQ
Tel: 01472 822270
Go Dance Studios
Tamer Court
Church Lane
SLEAFORD NG34 7DE
Tel: 01529 300930
**Stevenson School of
Dancing**
Above 513 Grimsby Road
CLEETHORPES DN35 8AN
Tel: 01472 601069

London
A.C.W. Dance Studio
Office only:
Garden Flat
20a Melrose Road
SOUTHFIELDS SW18 1NE
Tel: 020 8871 0890
www.acwdancestudio.com

Central London Dance
13 Blandford Street
W1U 3DF
Tel: 020 7224 6004
Dancewise
1st Floor
370 Footscray Road
NEW ELTHAM SE9 2AA
Tel: 020 8294 1576
www.dancewise.co.uk
**Flynn School of
Dancing**
40 Jago Close
PLUMSTEAD SE18 2TY
Tel: 01322 381070
Footsteps Stage School
(Chingford Loughton and
Chigwell)
Tel: 020 8500 6943
www.footstepsdance
school.com
**Linda Fountain School
of Dancing**
6 Voss Court
STREATHAM SW16 3BS
Tel: 020 8679 3040
J. B.'s Dance Studio
566 Romford Road
MANOR PARK E12 2AF
Tel: 07715 172624
Bruce Smith Studio
Lacey Hall
Hazelwood Lane
PALMERS GREEN N13 6DE
Tel: 01920 468857/07702
188368

Greater Manchester
A Touch of Class
139 High Street
Little Lever
BOLTON BL3 1LX
Tel: 01204 861242
Danceland
55 Bridgewater Street
Little Hulton
WORSLEY M38 9ND
Tel: 0161 703 9577
**Granada School of
Dancing**
St.Matthews Road (above
Conservative Club)
Edgeley
STOCKPORT SK3 9AM
Tel: 0161 480 6588
Parkfield Dance Centre
56 Eastwood Road
NEW MOSTON M40 3TF
Tel: 0161 682 4172
Sandham's Dance Studio
9a Peel Street
Farnworth

BOLTON BL4 8AA
Tel: 01204 795130
www.sandhams.co.uk
Village Dancentre
9 Park Road Hale
ALTRINCHAM WA15 9NL
Tel: 0161 928 9705

Merseyside
**Debonaires at the
Regency**
84 Prescot Road
ST HELENS WA10 3TY
Tel: 01744 759466
www.debonairesatthe
regency.com
**The New Regency Dance
Centre**
c/o 35 Hill School Road
ST HELENS WA10 3BH
Tel: 01744 21061
Silhouette Dance Club
29 Hillbray Avenue
ST HELENS WA11 7DL
Tel: 01744 20136
www.silhouette-dance
club.co.uk
**Pat Thompson Dance
Centre**
110 Northway
Maghull
LIVERPOOL L31 1EF
Tel: 0151 526 1056/526 2010

Norfolk
Connaught Dance Centre
1 Laxton Close
ATTLEBOROUGH NR17 1QY
Tel: 01953 455500
**Miller Dance and
Performing Arts Centre**
Units 1–3 Ropemakers Row
NORWICH NR3 2DG
Tel: 01603 488249
www.millerdance.co.uk
**Tempo Schools of
Dancing**
55 Mallard Way
Bradwell
GREAT YARMOUTH NR31 8LX
Tel: 01493 665558

Northamptonshire
Margo's Dance Centre
204 Windmill Avenue
KETTERING NN15 7DG
Tel: 01536 312002
Tempo Dance Studio
Bath Road, Tailby House
KETTERING NN16 8NL
Tel: 01536 723656
www.tempodancestudio.co.uk

Nottinghamshire

Ann Culley School of Dance
26 Main Street
PAPPLEWICK NG15 8FD
Tel: 0115 963 3428/07711
946335

The L.A. School of Dance
13 Cheddar Close
Rainworth
MANSFIELD NG21 0HX
Tel: 01623 796431/07984
079568

Ray Needham School of Dance
9 Douglas Crescent
CARLTON NG4 1AN
Tel: 0115 841 1779/07973
939378
www.rayneedham.co.uk

Oxfordshire

Abingdon Dance Studios
59 Swinburne Road
ABINGDON OX14 2HF
Tel: 01235 520195
www.abingdondance.co.uk

Sarah Ayers School of Dancing
20 Wytham View
Eynsham
OXFORD OX29 4LU
Tel: 01865 881208

Somerset

Davies School of Dance
12 The Hedges
St Georges
WESTON SUPER MARE
BS22 7SY
Tel: 01934 521338
www.davies-school-of-dance.co.uk

Langport Dance Centre
Bonds Farm
WEARNE (nr Langport)
TA10 0QQ
Tel: 01458 250322

Belinda Orford
Wayside Shepperdine Road
Oldbury Naite
BRISTOL BS35 1RJ
Tel: 01454 415346

PJ's Dance Academy
c/o 8 Meadow Drive
WESTON SUPER MARE
BS24 8BB
Tel: 01934 823948/ 07855
827464

Staffordshire

Flair Dance Academy
60 Etchinghill Road

RUGELEY WS15 2LW
Tel: 01889 579558

Shaftesbury School of Dancing
48 Palmers Green
Hartshill
STOKE ON TRENT ST4 6AP
Tel: 01782 618180
www.shaftesburydance.com

Suffolk

Lait Dance Club
St Matthew's Hall
Clarkson Street
IPSWICH IP1 2JD
Tel: 01473 215543
www.laitdanceclub.co.uk

Miller Dance and Performing Arts Centre
58 Bridge Road
Oulton Road
LOWESTOFT NR32 3LR
Tel: 01502 573000
www.millerdance.co.uk

Sussex

Crawley Dance Academy
3 Tushmore Avenue
Northgate
CRAWLEY RH10 8LF
Tel: 01293 612538

Tyne & Wear

Newcastle Dance Centre
36–38 Grainger Park Road
NEWCASTLE UPON TYNE
NE4 8RY
Tel: 0191 273 9987
www.newcastledance
centre.co.uk

Warwickshire

DancinTime
Terpsichore Cottage
81 Alcester Road
STUDLEY B80 7NJ
Tel: 01527 852178

Jonstar School of Dancing
22 Gibson Crescent
BEDWORTH CV12 8RP
Tel: 024 7631 6592

West Midlands

Boscott's Dance Club
5 Long Wood
BOURNEVILLE B30 1HT
Tel: 0121 459 9167

Broadway Dance Centre
42 Livingstone Road
Perry Barr
BIRMINGHAM B20 3LL
Tel: 0121 356 4663

Inspire School of Dance
11 Alverley Road
Daimler Green
COVENTRY CV6 3LH
Tel: 024 7659 3359

Touch of Class Dancentre (incorporating The Midland Stage School of Performing Arts)
Holloway Hall
Court Passage
off Priory Street
DUDLEY DY1 3EX
Tel: 01384 235999/07970
889251
www.freewebs.com/
touch-of-class-dancentre

Worcestershire

Catshill Dance Centre
Gibb Lane Catshill
BROMSGROVE B61 0JP
Tel: 01527 873638

Yorkshire East

Lacey School of Dancing
17 Grassdale Park
BROUGH HU15 1EB
Tel: 01482 666863

Lyndels Dancing Club
3 The Avenue
Melrose Street
HULL HU3 6EY
Tel: 01482 501248

Yorkshire North

Perry's Dancing
14 Haw Bank Court
SKIPTON BD23 1BY
Tel: 01756 794468 or 07900
285853

Playcraft Leisure School of Dancing
13 Kestrel Drive
Scotton
CATTERICK GARRISON DL9 3LX
Tel: 01748 830508

Yorkshire South

Joanne Armstrong School of Dancing
14 North End Drive
Harlington
DONCASTER DN5 7JS
Tel: 07979 758696
www.joannearmstrong.co.uk

Dentonia School of Dancing
Barnsley Road
Wombwell
BARNSLEY S73 8DJ
Tel: 01226 754684

Drapers Dance Centre
High Street
Beighton
SHEFFIELD S20 1ED
Tel: 0114 269 5703

Helen Neill School of Dance
41 Barnsley Road
Penistone
SHEFFIELD S36 8AD
Tel: 07771 610868

Yorkshire West

The D. M. Academy
The Studios
Briggate
SHIPLEY BD17 7BT
Tel: 01274 585317
www.dmacademy.co.uk

Horsforth Dance Academy
44 Hawksworth Avenue
GUISELEY
LEEDS LS20 8EJ
Tel: 01943 875894

Darren Peters Dance Centre
(Schools in Halifax, Thornton and Wilsden)
Tel: 07879 447106

Shandaw School of Dance
Serendipity Cottages
107–109 Gilstead Lane
Gilstead
BINGLEY BD16 3LH
Tel: 01274 510612
www.shandaw.co.uk

Wakefield Dance Group/ Wakefield City Slickers
82 Walton Lane
Sandal
WAKEFIELD WF2 6HQ
Tel: 01924 256624
www.members.lycos.co.uk/
davidherries/index.htm

The Windsor School of Dancing
5 Willow Street
Girlington
BRADFORD BD8 9LT
Tel: 01274 488961
www.windsorballroom.co.uk

York Dance Studios
8 Radcliffe Road
Milnsbridge
HUDDERSFIELD HD3 4LX
Tel: 01484 643120
yorkdance.co.uk

Scotland

Johnny & Eleanor Banks
13 Paisley Avenue
EDINBURGH EH8 7LB
Tel: 0131 6613447

Ms N Clark
61 Balnagowan Drive
GLENROTHES
Fife KY6 2SJ
Tel: 01592 772685

John & Charlotte Comrie
76 Balmoral Avenue
Balmoral Gardens
Glenmavis
AIDRIE ML6 0PY

**Andrew Cowan School
of Dance**
Community Central Hall
304 Maryhill Road
GLASGOW G20 7YE
Tel: 0141 6342129

Dees Dancing
PO Box 5456
GLASGOW G77 5LN
Tel: 0141 639 8300
www.deesdancing.co.uk

David Johnston
47 Polmont Road
Lauriestone
FALKIRK FK2 9QS
Tel: 01324 623007

Star Ballroom
10 Burnside Street
DUNDEE
Tel: 01382 611388

Christine Stevenson
(Various venues)
24 Ashgillhead Road
Larkhall
MOTHERWELL ML9 3AS
Tel: 01698 887296

**Diane Swan Ballroom
Dance Studio**
72 Balnagask Road
ABERDEEN, AB11 8RE
Tel: 01224 876444

Warrens
(Various Glasgow venues)
Tel: 0141 942 7670

Wales

Dance Kingdom
Pharaoh House
Station Yard
New Dock Road
LLANELLI SA15 2EF
Tel: 01554 771543
dancekingdom.co.uk

Edwards Studio of Dance
Victoria House

Andrews Road
Llandaff North
CARDIFF CF14 2JP
Tel: 01222 575487 or 01222
843120

New Cottage Dance Centre
Ystrad-Mynach
HENGOED CF82 7ED
Tel: 01443 815909

Richards School of Dance
144 Rhys Stret
Trealaw
TONYPANDY CF40 2QF
Tel: 07929 079403

DANCEWEAR

Chrisanne
Chrisanne House
14 Locks Lane
MITCHAM
Surrey CR4 2JX
Tel: 08640 5921
Fax: 08640 2106.
www.chrisanne.co.uk

Dance Naturals
Vua C. Varisco
6 – Zona Artigianale
35010 PERAGA DI VIGONZA
(Padova)
Italy
Tel: +39 0498935140
Fax: +39 0498935160
www.dancenaturals.com

**Dancesport International
Ltd**
The Courtyard
Aurelia Road
CROYDON CR0 3BF
Tel: 020 8665 7542

Glamour Gear
7 Norwich Road
IPSWICH IP1 2ET
Tel: 01473 289863
www.glamourgear.
co.uk

**International Dance
Supplies**
Harlequin House
Forde Court, Forde Road
NEWTON ABBOT
Devon TQ12 4BT
Tel: 01626 363232

Lazatrax
7 Woodstock Crescent
Dorridge
SOLIHULL
West Midlands B93 8DA
Tel/Fax: 01564 779267
Mobile: 07901 816233

**Stephen Martin
Dancewear**
PO Box 125
THORNTON CLEVELEYS
FY5 4WD
Tel: 01253 857369

Sapiel
Via Augusto 39 – 04011
APRILIA
Italy
Tel: +39 06 93748527
Fax: +39 06 9303560
www.sapiel.com

Supadance International Ltd
159 Queens Road
BUCKHURST HILL IG9 5BA
Tel 020 8505 8888

Shoes

Elite Dance Wear
Tel: 01476 572210
Fax/answerphone 0146
575600
elite-dancewear.co.uk.

Freed of London Ltd
www.freedoflondon.com

Supadance
80-82 Infirmary Road
SHEFFIELD
South Yorkshire S6 3DD
Tel: 0114 279 5979
Fax: 0114 279 5989
www.supadancesheffield.co.uk

Duo Dance
11 Half Moon Lane
Herne Hill
LONDON SE24 9JU
Tel: 020 7274 4517
Fax: 020 7733 4924
www.duodance.co.uk

Equity Shoes Ltd
42 Western Road
LEICESTER LE3 0GQ
Tel: 0116 254 9313
Fax: 0116 255 3769

International Dance Shoes
11 Fingle Drive, i. o. Centre
Stonebridge
MILTON KEYNES MK13 0AT
Tel: 01908 319937
Fax: 01908 220719
www.internationaldance
shoes.com

Fabrics

Nevtex
Sales Office: 0115 959 8781
www.nevtwx.co.uk

Men's Suits

Arthur Ashmore
Tel/Fax: 01384 255729
Mobile: 07712 091887
www.arthurashmore
tailors.co.uk

Ron Gunn
398 Leabridge Road
Leyton
LONDON E10 7DY
Tel: 020 8539 7075
Fax: 020 8539 7076

Index

Page numbers in *italic* refer to the illustrations

Acknowledgements

The publishers and authors would like to thank the following schools of dance, for their co-operation and supply of models for the step-by-step photography in this book: J.B.'s Dance Studio, King's Palais of Dance, Spotlight DanceWorld, Western Dance Centre and Wright Rhythm. All these schools are members of the IDTA (see page 250–1 for full details). Thanks also to Mr B. Perry of J.B.'s Dance Studio in Manor Park for providing the location for the dance photography, to Ross Mitchell of Dance and Listen Limited for the CD music (www.dance andlisten.com), and especially to the dancers:

Foxtrot: Kieran Smith and Kelly Neville
Waltz: Lee Delf and Kelly Dall
Cha Cha Cha: Barry Perry and Chris Jaques
Quickstep: Brenda and Clive Phillips
Rock 'n' Roll and Jive: Carl Webb and Emma Lee
Samba: Ben Petters and Jenna Fricker
Salsa: Kyle Magee and Lisa Russell
Tango: Katrina Eastabrook and Darren Coman
Rumba: Joe Nichols and Natalie Hassan
Disco/Freestyle: Kieran Smith and Shelly Tomlinson

Photo credits
Advertising Archives p. 50
BBC pp. 23, 51, 53, 72–3, 98, 118–19, 209
British Rail p.22
Corbis: pp.11 (Swim Ink 2, LLC), 15, 20–1, 74
(Bettmann/Corbis), 75 (Hulton-Deutsch Collection), 99,
168 (Peter Williams), 208, 237 (Bettmann/Corbis)
David Garten pp.206–7
Getty Images pp. 2, 6–7, 10, 13, 48–9, 96–7, 132–3, 148–9,
151, 222–3, 236
The Kobal Collection: pp. 120 (MGM), 121 (Paramount),
152 (RKO), 153 (20th Century Fox), 166–7 (Cannon),
169 (Mandalay Entertainment), 190–1 (MGM), 192 (Metro),
193 (Universal), 234–5 (Paramount)
Lebrecht Music & Arts pp. 11, 12
Lyndon Wainwright pp. 9, 14
All other photographs by Christopher H. D. Davis.

CD music credits
'Getting To Know You' (Rodgers, Hammerstein)
Williamson Music
'Sam' (Farrar, Marvin, Black) Rondor Music
'Pata Pata' (Makeba, Ragovoy) Peter Maurice Ltd
'Diamonds Are A Girl's Best Friend' (Robin, Styne) Dorset
Brothers Music USA
'Runaround Sue' (Di Mucci, Maresca) MCA Music Ltd
'Iko Iko' (Hawkins, Hawkins, Johnson, Thomas, Jones,
Jones, Jones) Carlin Music Corp. / Melder Publishing Co.
'She Knows That She Wants To' (Weimar, Wilson)
Copyright Control 2001 Dance And Listen Limited.
'Perfidia' (Dominguez) Milton-Leeds
'Can You Feel The Love Tonight?' (John, Rice) Wonderland
Music Co. Ltd.

Music provided by Ross Mitchell from the catalogue of
Dance And Listen Limited (www.danceandlisten.com)